Mystical Journeys and Sacred Initiations

Your Royal Highness
The Princess of Wales

∞

SUSIE TAMIM

Love and Light

Susie Tamim

Mystical Journeys and Sacred Initiations

Email: tamimsusie0@gmail.com

Print ISBN: 978-1-66789-400-3

eBook ISBN: 978-1-66789-401-0

The Hashemite Kingdom of Jordan, Department of the National Library

Deposit Number: (2023/9/4958) First Edition

altaj
press

Printed in Jordan by Al Taj Press - 2023

Email: info@altajpress.com

Tel: +962-799999434

In loving memory of my mother

Susan McArthur

CONTENTS

ACKNOWLEDGEMENTS

Special thanks are owed to many near and far for their continuous friendship, love and support as I was writing this book. In particular, a big thank you to: my twin sister, Tudy Williamson, for her beautiful painting of the blessed Muhammad Tree that I have used for the cover of this book; my editor, Jacky Sawalha; my friend, Rania Kurdi, for writing the foreword; and to my Reiki sisters. Special thanks are also owed to the following for their kind permission to quote: Manar Amin, Anya, Cheaya, Diana Cooper, Patricia Cori, Firas Fanous, Ziad and Shireen Hamzeh, Dr Nisreen, Dr Shirley Al Jabi, Louise Liggins, Robin Lown, Jennifer McKenzie, Roger Naylor, Donna Soudani and Ginny Toukan. Thanks also to Omar Sawalha for use of his photo of the night sky in Wadi Rum. But most of all, my deepest gratitude goes to my loving husband Amin, without whose endless patience and support of my work, I would never have been able to walk the path I have come to accept as my own.

FOREWORD

IN THE SUMMER OF 2002, I had just accepted an exciting offer to co-host the Pan Arab version of the singing talent TV show, *Pop Idol,* in Lebanon, when my mother introduced me to Susie Tamim, a Reiki Grand Master. I was immediately drawn to her charming personality and the beautiful, calming energy of her home. It was the perfect grounding I needed to balance the whirlwind journey into stardom and motherhood that was to come. I have been lucky to witness her amazing spiritual journey, and even after the passing of my mother a few years ago, Susie has remained a close friend. Little did I know back then that I would be the one to narrate the audio version of her first book, *Only Time Will Tell,* and would be writing the foreword to this exciting sequel, *Mystical Journeys and Sacred Initiations.*

I remember Susie's astonishment when she received a message from her late mother, told to her through a medium, that she had more to tell and needed to write again. This time, it all happened so quickly with the presence of her mother's spirit supporting her throughout the writing process. *Mystical Journeys and Sacred Initiations* transported me to so many different worlds as I read through each new chapter of Susie's wild adventures. The wonders, mysteries and ceremonies practised in each place she visits, are described in a way that makes me want to see them for myself and jump on a plane immediately. From UFO sightings and walking the Great Wall of China, to sacred ceremonies in Machu Picchu and spiritual blessings at the Great Pyramid, Susie is fearless as she embraces each new challenge. I also find myself appreciating Jordan in a completely different way when I see it through her eyes. There are layers and layers to discover and the book would make the perfect guide to anyone looking to visit and experience the true mysteries and gems hidden in the country.

I will end with the words Susie said when she was a guest on my podcast, Breaking Free. She explained that this book will make people wake up, and that if we listen to our inner voices, we can be guided to do what we have to do in this lifetime. I hope this book awakens in you a deeper understanding of your own true purpose.

Rania Kurdi, *Actress, podcaster & confidence coach*
https://www.raniakurdi.com/podcast

PREFACE

September 2020

THE COVID-19 PANDEMIC WAS RAGING throughout the world and I seemed to be in a year-long state of lockdown; looking after my spiritual well-being became my daily focus. And so, during a morning meditation session in my healing room, I connected to my higher-self – my inner voice – which came through strongly and told me to put my first book, *Only Time Will Tell*, online for free. I wondered why I had to deal with a book I had written 15 years ago. Yet, it made sense, as people are spiritually awakening and are more open-minded to enlightenment as they seek answers and deeper meaning to happenings in the world today.

A few days after I put my book online, I sent a copy to renowned British medium, Jennifer Mackenzie, whom I had met in Jordan in 2004. I received a message from Jennifer, who said that she spent the last two hours being "magically entertained." She also said, "You know there's still more to come," and mentioned that my story would open doors for me and give others the courage to go on. And then she typed, "I have a Susan with me. Is she your mother?" "Yes," I replied. "She's telling me to tell you, 'did you really think you have finished? Get out that computer or pen and paper. My goodness there is loads yet to tell, my lovely Susie'." Then Jennifer added, "She also said she's so proud of you and she's standing behind you as you write your second book."

This is the reason why I began to write *Mystical Journeys and Sacred Initiations*. I surprised myself with this second book; I had no intention of writing again, as I don't consider myself a writer. Yet, it was the sign from my beloved mother that I needed for the inspiration and guidance that produced this book.

I honestly felt her spirit close to me whilst I was writing. I knew she was there, as I felt a light touch on the top of my crown chakra and movement in my hair. Her reassuring presence allowed me to recall the details of events that I had forgotten and guided me about what to include. Now I have finished, I am sad to say that my mother's presence has served its purpose and moved on.

I was also saddened to learn of the passing of Jennifer Mackenzie on 11th January 2021. For me to reconnect with Jennifer online in September 2020, after a period of fifteen years, and to receive a final message from my mother through her was the sign I needed to write this book. I am a great believer in divine timing. Signs are all around us if we care to look, so join me as we share this journey together.

May Jennifer's beautiful soul rest in eternal peace.

Love and light
Susie Tamim
Amman, Jordan
January 2023

PROLOGUE

Meeting Robin – the Palmist

IT WAS THE WINTER OF 2013 and I was in the UK to visit my friend, Donna. While I was there, we attended the annual 'Mind Body Spirit Festival' held in Brighton, an easy trip from Donna's house. I signed up for the workshop held by therapist and healer, Diana Cooper, which she called: 'Accelerated Journey to Ascension'. It was a deeply uplifting and soul-healing workshop, which set the tone for the rest of my trip. Over breakfast one morning, Donna surprised me, "How would you like to go and see a top palmist and channeller?" I nearly choked on my tea! I was excited to go for one simple reason: I cannot read for myself.

Donna made an appointment the next day with renowned Master Palmist, Robin Lown. When we arrived, Robin welcomed us into his home and sat us down in the lounge. I asked him if I could record the session, so I could relax and listen instead of taking notes. "No problem," he said, "The session will take one hour." He took one look at me and said, "I don't know why you have come to me! You should be reading me, not me reading you!" I just smiled and said nothing.

I held out my hands and Robin began by telling me, "I see you will go to China in 2017." He explained that I have an incredible memory loop in my headline, which means that I collect memories that are very deeply rooted. "It's incredible," he said while looking at my right hand, "this memory loop is often seen on the hands of people who are very good writers or people who tell very good stories."

I could not believe what Robin had just told me, as I had written my autobiography, Only Time Will Tell, a few years ago. He also said that I had an incredible storage box, bigger than most people, as it showed in both hands. He continued, "So, therefore, in a sense, storing emotions is something you are able to do. You may not always want to access them because of difficulties like pain and suffering, call it what you like." He also told me that there was 'a very big hit' fairly early in my life, which indicates grief. That was when my mother died when I was 13 years old.

He continued, "You have travelled much and you understand different cultures and other places on the earth." He was right again because I worked as a flight attendant and had travelled worldwide. "There's a calmness about your nature, which indicates that you accept people from all parts of life and on every level, no matter who they are or stand for, even if he's a dustman or a king. You treat them all the same and you don't pass judgment on anybody." I explained to Robin that living in a Muslim country taught me to respect other people's religion and culture. "What I like about your hands is that you have learnt to have acceptance without judgment, but I feel people didn't understand you. This is because you are basically non-materialistic. It wouldn't matter if you slept in a Bedouin tent or Buckingham Palace! It doesn't bother you where you sleep. You would sleep on a washing line if you had to! I don't know how you do it! Well, that's the way you have always been, that's quite unusual!" I chuckled and had to agree with him.

Robin then asked about the date of my birth – 29 November – as he was "pretty much done with my character." He told me the first part of my birth chart is 22 and that if I went to a numerologist, they would say, "This is a bit different." The 11th month means 'the student', so the 22 and 11 meant that I am the student and master of my own life. He was correct again, as my education was life, especially losing my mother at such an early age and working to survive independently from the age of 16.

He mentioned how this was rather an interesting concept, "you can be somewhere or doing something and you feel you are observing yourself. You can be a fly on the wall, looking at all that's going on and not really being there." He went on to explain how this was possible. "You have the ability to be in two places at once and you can remove yourself out of a situation, which is a rather strange way of being. Evidently, this has happened to the masters of old, who used to arrive somewhere and then see the whole picture by taking themselves out of body, like they are astral travelling. I know it sounds rather weird, but you have that ability too. Now I know I am talking to somebody who has the ability to be a little bit different to everyone around. I don't mean to be rude, but you couldn't really get started in life until you actually fell apart."

He was so right. When I was much younger, I suffered from depression until I got a message from my mother at the Spiritual Association in London, who told me to pull myself together and to stop feeling sorry for myself. It was then that I began to listen to my mother's messages from the spirit world.

Robin continued, "You had nothing keeping you in England as your mother died when you were 13, and by the time you got to 16-17, the wind could have taken you anywhere like a butterfly and you didn't mind where you went." He had interpreted my feelings so well at that age because all I could think was, 'just take me anywhere, spirit.'

Robin looked down at my left hand and told me he could see me connected to foreign lands and countries between the ages of 31 to 39. "And when you were 40, something went 'poof'. There was an opportunity for a new life," he continued, "and what was wonderful at that time was that your life really did take off at certain times. It's like being whisked off, like a hovercraft or an airplane, into a completely different environment.

That 'poof' was when I went to live in Jordan in 1981 to work as a flight attendant for the national carrier, Royal Jordanian. Shortly after, I gave up my job when I got married at the age of 40 and began my spiritual journey

Robin then noticed on my right palm a square that he said indicates there were some restrictions in my work, "Because people didn't understand you and the work you did. The people you mixed with and were connected to, didn't understand you either. You actually had some status." He also told me that sometimes people would ask deep and personal questions, but that I have the ability to give understated answers and not give away much personal information. Robin continued, "I am not being rude to you, but people would say, 'who is she? What is she doing here?' So in a sense, you were kind of strange to people around you in Jordan, but they will all come back to you in the end. Just believe in yourself; you have been given a gift from God." Robin was right again because now I feel I am respected for my work and I am more aware of the gift God gave me: to help people find their way in this life or the afterlife.

My one-hour session was up and I was so happy with my reading. I was also curious, as he was the first person to mention I would go to China; he would not be the last. This trip to the UK turned into a wholly personal journey of inner discovery and validation, one more stepping-stone of my life that Robin so accurately described. He was right; that gift from God I humbly accept as my mission in life.

Chapter 1

AMMARIN BEDOUIN CAMP, WADI AL AMTI

A Place where Heaven meets the Earth

IN THE YEAR 2001, MY FRIENDS and I decided to visit the Ammarin Bedouin Camp, part of the Petra Archaeological Park, in an area called Baidha (also known as 'Little Petra' with a passage through the rocks, called 'Siq al Barid'). It is one of the most beautiful and spiritual areas in Jordan.

Situated in Wadi Al Amti – the place where Heaven meets the Earth – the Ammarin Bedouin Camp was established in 2000 by Ziad Hamzeh and the local community cooperative. It was set up to be a sustainable income-generating project that would benefit approximately two hundred families of the local and original Bedouin inhabitants of Wadi Al Amti. Baidha itself is an archaeological site located 10km north of the famed ancient Nabatean kingdom of Petra. The energy of Baidha is exceptional and has a powerful spiritual dynamic. You can feel the yin–yang energies that are in balance in this spiritual place. When we talk about the 'spirit' of nature, we mean its essence or consciousness that Earth is communicating to us – a neutral zone that can be considered a sacred and spiritual space – and it has nothing to do with djinn. A stay in this hallowed place can be regarded as a spiritual retreat and a safe space for each person to embrace a higher dimension of awareness and well-being.

In anticipation of this spiritual journey, we set off for Baidha and arrived three hours later. As we settled into our goat hair tents, a young Bedouin boy arrived with a tray of glasses filled with sweet mint tea, which he offered as a welcoming gesture to the camp. We were at peace. The tranquillity and manifest-healing energy of our surroundings embraced us in one of the oldest places of recorded history.

After dinner, our guide suggested that we walk to a special area that he called 'fairyland'. We walked ahead bare-footed on the sand, not knowing where we were going and all I could feel was a tingling sensation throughout my body; I was at peace within my being. We eventually reached a place where we were asked to sit around on the rocks. Our guide began to relate amazing stories about the metaphysical aspects of this special place, set deep within the Sharah mountain range. He talked to us about ley-lines that were present within the Petra region and how they create a vortex of energy. The best explanation I was given was that these ley-lines are like acupuncture meridians in the human body and exist on a larger scale within the Earth.

Ammarin Bedouin Camp, Wadi Al Amti, Petra Archaeological Park

Ley-lines are tracks that stretch across the landscape and can be 1-100 kilometres long. There is much speculation as to their precise meaning or purpose, but nowadays, it is believed that they are great sources of power generated by shifting magnetic fields along these tracks. There are locations on the Earth that are filled with special energy and ley-lines, such as Petra, but also predominantly at Stonehenge, the Pyramids of Egypt, Machu Picchu of Peru, Mount Everest and Sedona in America, to name a few.

We were so fascinated by the talk on ley-lines that we had not noticed that the sun had begun to set, until we were engulfed in darkness. It was the perfect moment to meditate under a tableau of a star-lit sky. After a while, I felt a strange force pulling on my rings to take them off my finger. I tried so hard to stop it, but it happened so quickly. "They took my rings!" I screamed out loud in disbelief. Everyone jumped up, trying to see if they could find them in the sand. "What am I going to tell my husband?" I cried when all of a sudden, one of my rings rose out of the sand like magic and Ziad managed to catch it for me. However, the other ring was gone forever. Our guide smiled knowingly. "The benevolent fairies, Susie, they took your ring as they gave you energy in return," he said. I did not understand this at the time, but a few years later, it made sense when I received a message from the spirit world through my Bedouin client.

The next morning, we all woke to the smells of bread baking over an open fire and the sweet smell of mint tea wafting through our tent; it was the sign that breakfast was served. The aromas, colours and tastes of traditional Arabic food soon transformed my gloomy mood making it a perfect ending to a memorable visit. Despite losing my ring, I felt different that morning; a sense of awakening and a deeper understanding of my life's work left me feeling at peace and ready for another mystical journey.

Chapter 2

SEDONA, ARIZONA, USA

"Beneath the endless beauty beats a healing heart."[1]

SEDONA IS A CITY IN ARIZONA, in the southwestern United States of America, known as one of the most beautiful places on Earth, for good reason. Surrounded by Yucca trees, cacti and grand red rocks that tower over this ancient land, Arizona is also home to the Grand Canyon. However, its "beating healing heart" is found in Sedona, a sacred and powerful place that people visit in search of the vortex experience; a place where the earth seems alive with a mysterious energy that inspires, recharges, uplifts, soothes and restores. Vortexes are sites with enhanced energy that emanate from the rocks that people visit to facilitate prayer, meditation, enlightenment and mind-body-soul healing;[2] a place where the soul can journey for answers. Drive quickly through Sedona and you may not feel much impact. But if you stay for a while, you can focus on connecting with this spiritual energy by meditating in silence and being at one with your higher self.

My friend Ginny and I have always wanted to visit Sedona. And so in November of 2002, I flew to Boston, where I met up with Ginny and her friend Pam, and the three of us flew to Phoenix. On arrival, we stayed at the Enchantment Resort in Sedona, which is built right next to a vortex site at

---

[1] Roger Naylor, Arizona author and travel writer. (www.rogernaylor.com)
[2] https://visitsedona.com/what_is_a_vortex_handout_(002).pdf

Boynton Canyon. We could not wait to explore the area and decided to start with the Grand Canyon, one of the Seven Wonders of the World. It was a phenomenal experience to see such magnificent scenery from the window of the small 4-seater private plane that we had hired. The large, lush pine trees thriving amidst a desert landscape were a joy to behold. On the way back, it was only then that I noticed how quiet and frightened Ginny appeared to be; she looked petrified. Our plane had hit a few air pockets and swerved from side to side, and even though I had experience flying through air pockets, I even felt a bit nervous at times. This was, of course, much different from my days as a flight attendant. Ginny said, "I didn't want to frighten you, Susie, but the biggest mistake I made was to read an article in the hotel magazine, which said many planes and helicopters crashed going into the Grand Canyon because of the high winds between the mountains." I was relieved she had not told me beforehand, even though I knew intuitively that all would be well.

The next day, we boarded a helicopter for the first time in our lives and flew all the way down to the floor of the Grand Canyon, where it landed. I was amazed that I wasn't frightened at all, especially as I had to overcome a fear of heights my whole life. I loved every moment of it, as I stood in awe on the edge of the Colorado River. I was totally absorbed in the positive energy that was all around as we boarded the boat to cruise this mighty river. The air was so fresh and clean that I breathed in this pure oxygen that filled my lungs to over-flowing. We did not talk, as we were immersed in the beautiful sounds and sights of nature while the boat sailed silently along the river; a soothing change from the loud noises of the helicopter.

Eventually, it was time to head back to the hotel. It was a memorable day and I thought that the word 'Grand' was inadequate to describe this magnificent canyon. We turned in early, as we had a busy schedule in the morning to visit the vortex sites. Our hotel was located in the spiritual heart of Sedona, surrounded by towering red rock walls, known as the Boynton Canyon.

The resort combined the rugged grandeur of the southwest landscape and Native American culture with plenty of activities and panoramic views of the red rock formations – it was breathtaking. After breakfast, we headed out along the easy route to Cathedral Rock, one of the most scenic vortex sites in Sedona, as we did not think we could handle the challenging climb of more than 650 feet up the rocks along the main route to Cathedral Rock. This vortex is said to have contemplative power that can enhance memories of past lives. It is a powerful, yet subtle form of energy that has a calming effect. With this in mind, we found a lovely spot to sit and meditate, and just before I went into a state of meditation, I stated, "I am ready to accept anything you want to give me." However, little did I know what the outcome of that statement would be when I engaged with the mighty vortex energy.

While I was meditating, I could not believe what I was seeing in a vision. I could see myself on a beautiful white stallion, as an indigenous Apache Indian chief. I could hear the sounds of tribal life; of drumbeats and people dancing and singing; I was looking down on the whole of Sedona. I vividly remember that I had a beautiful headdress filled with feathers of every colour. When I finally came back to earth and slowly came out of my meditative state, it took me a while to register what I had just witnessed. I realised that I had just experienced a past life as an Apache Indian chief; an experience that I will always remember.

Ginny had a vision of a beautiful tall angel, dressed in a long white robe, standing over her and blessing her. It is a well known fact that whoever goes to Cathedral Rock will have a past life vision, even if one thinks they are not intuitive. We asked Pam what she saw, only to learn that she was too frightened to meditate, as she was scared to see a past life and wasn't ready for the experience. She just kept her eyes open the whole time.

We continued to walk along the trail and came to the Chapel of the Holy Cross that had been built into the red rock cliffs of Sedona. This chapel is considered one of the seven man-made wonders of Arizona and I could see why; the building evoked a sense of awe that enhanced the spiritual experience. Inspired by the Empire State Building, it was commissioned by local rancher and sculptor Marguerite Brunswig Staude who once wrote, "The doors of this chapel will always be open to one and all, regardless of creed." [3]

Chapel of the Holy Cross, Sedona

As we walked around this serene space, we made our way to the top deck of the chapel. The view was captivating. As I looked out onto this mystical landscape, I was in complete harmony with nature and it reminded me of Wadi Rum back home in Jordan. Further along the trail, we arrived at the strong vortex energy site of Bell Rock, a towering natural rock formation that makes it easy to pinpoint. The scenic views from Bell Rock took my breath away, especially in the mornings when the sun rose over the mountains and lit up the

---

[3] https://chapeloftheholycross.com/history/

sandstone valley in a magic array of orange and red with a golden sheen; it warmed my soul. While I was there, I felt a constant tingling sensation throughout my being, which gave me the energy to trek around this magical place for hours. By the time we returned to our hotel at the end of the day, we felt energised, uplifted and at peace. As it was our last night, we took a dip in the jacuzzi on the terrace, and while we were gazing up at the night sky, we were treated to the most beautiful display of falling stars as if they were saying 'goodbye.'

When I tried to get out of bed the following morning, I could not stand up. "Ginny, Ginny, I can't walk straight!" I yelled. It was so loud I must have woken up all the guests in the hotel. It was frightening. "Why is this happening to me on the day I'm flying home?" And then I realised what I had asked for when meditating at Cathedral Rock. I thought that I should not have 'accepted anything you want to give me.' Even at the airport, I could not stand on my own, and Ginny and Pam had to explain what had happened to me to the customs official. "You must be psychic," he said. I was surprised. "How do you know I'm psychic? You must be psychic yourself to know this." He laughed, "Have you been staying at the vortexes? Because most psychic people can have this reaction." What I did not realise, however, is that the vortex energy would also amplify whatever I was feeling. It was this energy that hit me hard, especially as we slept on top of a vortex for a whole week. I felt that I was not within my body, half in and half out. I only later understood what the customs official meant because people who are in touch with their emotions and have developed their intuition and psychic ability, including energy healing such as Reiki and therapeutic touch, will consistently have a more potent experience in Sedona.

I felt quite anxious but did not want to worry Ginny, so I kept my feelings to myself. When we reached Boston, we visited Ginny's mother-in-law, who took one look at me and invited us to stay with her. When I looked at myself in the mirror, I was shocked. I looked different - even my eyes did not look like mine.

The next day, Ginny took me to a hospital nearby, where they gave me an MRI and checked my ears for vertigo. I had all the tests possible, but they could not find anything wrong with me. Then we went to settle the bill and because I was a 'foreigner,' I was charged $10,000. I was shocked to hear this, and I explained I was a tourist and I did not have that kind of money. I felt a wave of tears running down my face and asked if there was any way to reduce the cost. I offered to make payments monthly and they agreed. With that, we left and I prayed for a miracle. The next day, I boarded the flight home and when the plane landed in Amman, the flight attendant kindly got me a wheelchair to passport control and even collected my luggage. I did not take the wheelchair through the arrival lounge so as not to shock my husband. With all my strength, I gripped the handles of the trolley to allow me to walk out. I saw Amin waiting for me with a big smile on his face.

When we arrived home, he noticed I was swaying from side to side and could not walk straight. "What's wrong, Susie?" he asked with a worried look on his face. Then I had to tell him what had happened. Amin panicked; he cannot stand to see me ill at any time. So the next morning, he booked an appointment for me to see the doctor and all my x-rays were normal. The doctor gave me a neck brace to see if that would help, but it didn't. After a week, I just took the neck brace off. I intuitively knew it was not vertigo, so I continued giving myself hands-on Reiki healing energy every day.

After three months, I was still feeling spaced out when I received the bill from the American hospital, and to my great surprise, all I had to pay was $150. I was so relieved, as my prayers had been answered; it was a miracle and I gave thanks to God.

All the healings I gave myself daily made me feel at peace, despite feeling that part of me was down on earth and part of me felt like I was in another dimension. All my friends were shocked at how different I looked and I knew they were all very concerned for me.

The following week, I received a phone call from Firas, who asked if I could give him the Reiki Grand Master course.

We met the next day and I explained what happened to me in Sedona. "Wait a minute, Susie, I can help you. I'm a Karuna[4] Master Teacher, and I have a symbol that could ground you," he said. "Oh please do, I would do anything to feel normal again. I just hate the way I feel, it's quite frightening."

He sat me on a chair and as he was attuning me to the Karuna Reiki symbol, I began to feel a boost of energy that felt like a jolt from above and I almost fell to the floor; I felt centred, emotionally connected and balanced once more. I startled Firas, too, as he did not expect to see how disconnected I had become.

After the blessing, I felt I was finally grounded and back down on earth; I felt safe and normal again. My prayers were answered because God had sent Firas to me, which was the sign I needed. I believe that some people act like Earth Angels and come in and out of our lives for a reason. They come to help when called upon, and this was one of those times when I really needed help. As Firas had given me the Karuna Reiki Master Teacher symbols, in return, I taught him the Reiki Grand Master training course.

---

[4] Mikao Usui, a Japanese Buddhist priest and the father of Reiki as we know it today, introduced Reiki to the world in 1922. The word is composed of **rei,** which means *universal life* and **ki,** which means *energy.* Karuna Reiki is an extension of the Usui Reiki method. Karuna is a Sanskrit word, which means *compassionate action* and was developed by William L. Rand in 1989. Usui Reiki refers to the safe and holistic method of hands-on healing, while Karuna Reiki assists in clearing traumas from the physical body and in deeper understanding of one's mission in life. Usui Reiki and Karuna Reiki are both sources of God-given universal life force energy.

Chapter 3

CIRCLE OF FRIENDS

A FEW WEEKS LATER, I met Firas for coffee and we discussed establishing a 'Circle of Friends'[5]. This idea came about because of various 'days of well-being' that were being held in England at that time. Firas and I thought it would be an opportunity to do this in Amman, as many people were suffering the trauma of wars in our region. We felt the time was right to raise awareness and to bring spiritual enlightenment through workshops and lectures, as a means for holistic self-healing.

I gathered four friends to join us and in July 2003 we began to organise our first event at the Intercontinental Hotel Amman. It was a great success and we were truly taken by surprise at the influx of people who joined us for this event. It was only a matter of time before the next 'day of well-being' was set up at the same hotel over a period of two days in May 2004. These 'days of well-being' gave a platform to many people who were experts in alternative holistic healing methods, such as: Reflexology, Aromatherapy, Bach Flower Remedies, Acupuncture, Yoga, Tai Chi, Chi Gong, Reiki and many more.

As part of another activity, we thought of doing something different by bringing a top international clairvoyant and healer to offer a workshop. As Donna was going to England, I asked her if she could go to the Spiritual Association in London to see if she could find a clairvoyant who would visit Jordan.

Donna said, "Susie, something is telling me to take one of your Reiki leaflets with me." Knowing how intuitive Donna was, I agreed. In the meantime, I

---

[5] The Circle of Friends was established in Amman by: Salma Moghraby, Donna Soudani, Shireen Hijazzi, Salam Moghraby, Firas Fanous and Susie Tamim.

emailed a friend who was a member of the Spiritual Association and asked her if she knew of any good clairvoyants who would agree to take part in our event. She wrote back and recommended Jennifer Mackenzie, a world-renowned clairvoyant who gives private consultations, past life regression sessions, and healing. I immediately emailed Jennifer and asked if she would come to Jordan at any time. When Donna returned to Amman, she told our Circle of Friends that she had met with Jennifer Mackenzie at the Spiritual Association and handed over my leaflet, and had enquired if she would be interested to come to Jordan. Jennifer told her she was very busy, but would consider some time in 2005. I was completely taken aback, as I had not known that Donna had met with Jennifer.

A week later, Jennifer replied to my email and confirmed her interest, as she realised the person in the leaflet that Donna had given her, was me! It was a complete coincidence, or was it? Then I knew God was working through us, as Jennifer decided that this was a sign for her to visit Jordan, so she cancelled her trip to America and planned to visit Jordan instead in 2004.

One day, one of my clients gave me some beautiful candles with a Virgin Mary sticker all around the outside of the candle. When I finally burned the last candle in my healing room, I prayed, 'I'm sorry Mary, I have no more to burn on my altar for you.' A week went by and Lana, my client, rang me. "Susie, I have three CD tapes of American author, Caroline Myss, who is very spiritual and has written many books. Would you like them?" she asked. "I would love them. Thank you!" I replied. "Ok then, I will send my driver to your house." Within an hour the doorbell rang and I thought the driver had arrived and let him into the building. I told him to come to the fourth floor. As the lift arrived, I opened the front door but discovered there was no one there; however, I did hear someone coming up the stairs very slowly and breathing heavily, so I went down to meet him halfway and met an elderly white-bearded man with deep blue eyes, wearing a white *abayyah* (traditional long robe usually worn by men in the Arab world). I was taken aback by his appearance but felt he had an incredible energy that emanated from his aura. He greeted me and said, '*Assalamu alaykum*,' (peace be upon you) – a traditional greeting in Arabic. With a beaming smile, he handed me a package, turned around and left without another word.

When I went back upstairs to unwrap my gift, I could not understand what had just happened. Inside the bag were three Virgin Mary candles, just like the ones I had in my healing room. I rang Lana to thank her for the candles, and added, "I don't want to be ungrateful, but didn't you say you were going to send me some CDs?" "Yes, just a minute, Susie, I will ask my driver." When she came back she told me that her driver had not yet left the house. Then, who was the man who gave me the candles? I just assumed it must have been a divine gift from the spirit world and thought nothing more of the incident.

It was in March 2004 when Jennifer arrived at the airport and we met her directly off the plane. She took one look at Donna and I, and with a bright smile, she said, "I don't know why I've come with you two here!" Donna and I exchanged a quick glance, as we did not know what to make of that statement. We left the airport and headed to the home of Salma, who was kind enough to host Jennifer during her stay. Little did we realise what Jennifer meant when she greeted us at the airport. She had sensed that we were as psychic as she was, something that we were not fully aware of at that time. It was thanks to Jennifer's comment at the airport that day, which gave us the sign that we were on the right path.

The next day, Jennifer held a mediumship and healing session at Salma's house for about thirty people. She explained how the session would unfold, which was fairly straightforward. Jennifer began by saying, "When I work, I have a Chinese man who works through me to do the healing. So if anyone is squeamish or scared, please leave the room now." I looked around the room to see if anyone would leave, and no one did.

First, she picked a few people from the audience and gave them messages from passed loved ones in the spirit world. She pointed at me and said, "I have a Susan here, it's your mother, she's telling me to ask you if you got the three Virgin Mary candles she sent to you this morning?" I was speechless; tears began to roll down my cheeks and I could barely reply that I had, when Lana stood up and said, "Incredible! I can't believe what I'm hearing, as I am a witness," and she began to relate the story of her driver not being the one who brought me the candles. Everyone in the audience was amazed to hear this and stood up and applauded Jennifer. I knew then that the old man in the white *abayyah* with the bright blue eyes who had brought me the candles was an Earth Angel.

Jennifer then asked, "Is there anyone in the audience who would like to be healed?" I found my voice again and shouted out, "Yes, please!" as I had a very annoying ringing sound in my left ear. I went up to her and sat on a chair facing the audience. All I remember was a click of her fingers. It was like she hypnotised me while she did psychic surgery on my ear.

When it was all over, it took me a while to come around and all I could hear was clapping. My friend Margaret approached me and explained what she had just witnessed. "First, you see Jennifer standing at the side of you and her whole body started to shrink into a little old Chinese man. Her voice even changed into a man's voice. 'You poor child, you have not had an easy life,' the voice said, and he proceeded to bless you and worked on your ear for at least twenty minutes." Margaret then explained that when 'he' had finished working on me, the Chinese man changed back into Jennifer, and with a click of her fingers, I woke up. It was a unique experience for everyone but especially for me, as the ringing in my ear had gone.

The next morning, Firas kindly let Jennifer do readings at his office in Amman. I took the last appointment as we both agreed to give each other a reading. Jennifer told me, "Susie, I have a Thomas here." "Yes, that's my father," I replied. Jennifer continued, "He's telling me that he's very proud of you and loves the room with the pictures of flowers on the wall; it is a room full of positive energy." I was puzzled; which pictures with the flowers?

Then Jennifer went on and asked me, "Did you ever give healing to the late King Hussein?" I replied, "No, I have never met him personally, but I sent him daily Reiki distant healing when I heard he was seriously ill." I had always admired the way he cared for his people and country. Jennifer said, "Well he's here now! And he's thanking you for all the healings you gave him. He's smiling while telling me." I did not want to believe what I had just heard. "Well, tell him to help me," I said. "I want to see him today in front of me and then I will believe it's him."

While Salma drove me home from the session, a Range Rover with flashing red lights had overtaken us, but had to stop at the traffic lights. When we pulled up behind this car, I came face to face with the late King Hussein, literally; a poster of the late King smiling and waving had been stuck all over the back window of the car. Salma and I realised it was a profound sign, the one that I had asked for. I knew then that universal Reiki energy really does work distantly. I said a little prayer to thank God for showing me that with faith anything is possible.

When I returned home, I made myself a cup of tea and pondered on all that had happened that day, including my father's message about the room with the flowers in the pictures. I realised that he must have been referring to my healing room, so I went to check. As I entered the room, I glanced up instinctively at the seven pictures of the chakras that my friend Maria had painted long ago. It then dawned on me that each chakra was painted in the shape and colour of a flower; I had never noticed the flowers before. Thanks to my father's message from the spirit world, now I know.

Chapter 4

PERU AND MACHU PICCHU

The Sacred Symbol of the Incas

IT WAS SEPTEMBER 2008 AND I was in Dubai to do my spiritual work whilst staying with a friend. One Friday morning, while she was browsing the Internet, she came across a great offer for a trip to Peru. "Susie, how about going to Peru?" she said with a big cheeky grin. "Are you joking?" "No, I'm not," she replied. "Okay then, let's go!" I have always loved doing things on the spur of the moment and I had always wanted to visit Machu Picchu, a sacred symbol of the empire of the Incas.

A few days later, we arrived in Lima and met up with our guides and tourists from all over the world who had joined our group tour. We introduced ourselves, at least, I think we did, as we were so tired from the 24-hour flight that I was beginning to have double vision. After a good night's sleep, we had an early pickup for the short flight to Cusco, the capital of the Inca Empire.

We checked into our hotel in Cusco and met with our group at the reception. Our guides had important information to tell us: "Go and relax and breathe in the fresh mountain air so that you get used to the high altitude. This is because a lack of oxygen is the only thing that will prevent you having a great time." They also told us to drink cocoa tea leaves every morning to help our bodies adjust to the altitude, which can generally start affecting people at eight thousand feet or higher.

We then headed out to explore the Pisac Sunday Market, one of the most famous markets in the Cusco region, where you can find all kinds of indigenous handicrafts, including flutes, hand-knitted Alpaca wool sweaters and hats, backpacks, and little knitted figurines of animals in amazing colours. It was bursting with local vendors from the Quechua communities, and it was hard not to buy everything on display. I had never experienced such a vibrant and fascinating market, full of friendly and beautiful people wearing exquisite traditional clothes and famed bowler hats in all shapes and colours – a symbol of pride and identity for the women of the Peruvian highlands.

Walking around the town, we became immersed in a deeply spiritual culture; it always has been, even before the time of the Incas. We learnt about the strong sacred connection between the people of Peru and the three animals that make up the Trilogy in Incan beliefs:[6] the condor bird, the puma and the serpent. These three animals are symbolic of the three stages of Incan life: the condor represents the heavens as a messenger of the Gods; the puma represents the middle world of life on Earth as a symbol of power and strength; and the serpent represents the underworld and the beginning of new life.[7] Many people still believe that these animals play a significant role in their lives, which is why you will see them on various sculptures and buildings across the country. We also learnt about 'the chakana', an ancient carved symbol representing the Southern Cross constellation that the Incas adapted as the centre of their universe. More recently, the chakana has been referred to as the Inca Tree of Life. [8]

It is thought that the sacred city of Machu Picchu may have been designed around the image of the condor bird, with its wings stretching up the mountains into heaven. Inca buildings were designed in harmony with nature and the surrounding landscape to align with the sun and stars, particularly during the equinox and solstices. Even the layout of the town of Cusco is believed to have initially taken the shape of a puma when viewed from above.

---

[6] https://www.kuodatravel.com/the-inca-trilogy-the-condor-the-puma-and-the-serpent.
[7] https://theculturetrip.com/south-america/peru/articles/the-spiritual-importance-of-the-condor-puma-and-snake-in-peruvian-history/
[8] https://www.tourinperu.com/blog/chakana-inca-cross-symbol

The Trilogy

With this in mind, we set off to find an ideal place to rest. After an hour, we found the perfect, isolated spot. It was so peaceful and quiet. There was not a soul to be seen. We felt an overriding urge to connect to Mother Earth. We laid down flat on our backs on the ground, with our arms and legs outstretched, looking up at the clear blue sky, when to our amazement, we saw two condor birds flying high in the sky, circling directly above us. Even when we got up and walked back to the hotel, they stayed with us for quite a while. We were so lucky to see the condor bird, as this special animal spirit guide can help you to establish boundaries and to release negative emotions to help you feel energised. I felt this was no coincidence to experience this unique moment of bonding with nature. It was truly a blessing from the higher realm.

The next morning, we explored the largest structure built by the Incas, the Sacsayhuaman, a sacred fortress-temple complex constructed during the mid-fifteenth century that lies to the north of Cusco. It included many temples and stepped terraces, possibly for astronomical observations, and in particular, there was a temple dedicated to the sun god, Inti. This is one of the most mysterious places on Earth that blends harmoniously into the natural landscape. It is still used today to hold Inca-inspired ceremonies.

Me meditating

The Incas were master stonemasons, which can be seen by the unique stonework of the walls that are typical of Sacsayhuaman. I was astonished to learn how they achieved such perfect curves and angles with massive stone blocks, some up to four metres in height, put together without the use of mortar. It was an awesome sight.

The day had finally arrived when we left on a special visit to the world's highest lake, Titicaca, and I was filled with anticipation. According to mythology, it is at Lake Titicaca that the Creator God, Viracocha, the primary god of the ancient peoples of the Andes region, created the sun and the moon, the heavens and the earth during a time of darkness. It is said that as Viracocha wandered through the Southern Hemisphere, he taught men the art of civilisation, and then he crossed the Pacific Ocean, never to return.[9] I took a moment to gaze out over this vast expanse of blue water that meant so much to so many; it was awe-inspiring.

Around the lake, thousands of local inhabitants make their living by fishing in its icy waters, growing potatoes along its fertile edge, or herding llama and alpacas. The turquoise blue lake was the most sacred body of water in the Inca Empire and is now the natural separation between Peru and Bolivia.

We took a flotilla cruise on Lake Titicaca to the famed floating islands of the Uru people who live directly upon the great Mama Cocha, the Mother Lake, which, I heard, connects the 'angelic realms'[10] with the 'messengers of light'. I believe I was destined to visit this beautiful lake to absorb its sacred energy and to connect with the remarkable Uru people, the messengers of light of the Southern Hemisphere.

On arrival, our Uru host beckoned us to sit on ready-made, tightly bundled reed seats and gave us all a warm welcome. He showed us how they made the floating islands, their homes and boats – all with layers of dried totora reeds that are constantly maintained, as they tend to rot. The totora reeds grow along the banks of Lake Titicaca and provide a constant supply of food and medicine, as well as a refreshing tea when its flowers are in bloom.

It was fascinating to learn how people live on the great Mother Lake in harmony with nature. Some of the men from our group asked if they could experience staying the night on the floating island, and they accepted.

One of the Uru women showed us into her home, a cosy two-metre-wide room with a small, raised platform bed. She proudly showed us how she stored her belongings by hanging the beautifully coloured clothes, the few she had, on a nail on the wall, where she also hung a piece of material on which she had pinned small amounts of paper money. I was amazed and humbled by their

[9] Minster, Christopher. "Viracocha and the Legendary Origins of the Inca." ThoughtCo, Aug. 26, 2022, thoughtco.com/viracocha-and-legendary-origins-of-inca-2136321.
[10] https://www.crystalheaven.co.uk/angels/

simple lifestyle, as they were very happy and content, adapting so well to the changes of modern life. They showed us how they cooked their food on a heated stone so that the reeds don't catch fire, and how they use special toilets where the ground roots absorb the waste. They also used solar panels, which gave them electricity for lighting, televisions, and charging their mobile phones. I asked them about schooling for their children and I was told that the younger children are home-schooled by the Uru, while the older children continue their education on the mainland. It made me realise how much we take for granted and complain about the smallest things in our own lives.

The Uru people of Lake Titicaca

The following day, when the group arrived back at the hotel, they looked rather tired but happy, and they told us that their local hosts put on a lovely show for them and danced and played Peruvian music till the early hours of the morning. Their festive food included duck, catfish, trout and giant toads, all caught in the waters of Lake Titicaca. It was an experience that brought the two cultures together – the sharing of music and food – and it was one that they will never forget.

Inside the home of our Uru host

We walked along the shores of Lake Titicaca in the footprints of the deity Viracocha in his guise as a puma, who, it is said, emerged to inspect and bless his people and lands. His footprint is forever immortalised in stone. This ritualised walk took us through the mysterious 'spirit valley', adorned with strange stone formations in the likeness of people and animals, that led to the equally mysterious doorway carved into the rock face. Known as Aramu Muru, or the 'Gate of the Gods' by the locals, this doorway is believed by some to be a type of paranormal 'portal'. It is one of the most mystical rock formations to be found near Lake Titicaca.

When we arrived at Aramu Muru, the shaman guided us to walk, one at a time, towards the doorway and to face the wall with outstretched hands on the stone. I felt that this strange opening had something to do with the higher realms. As I faced the doorway, I felt a unique spirituality and a strange feeling as if my hands were going through the walls. When we walked back from the portal, the shaman then blessed all of us on our third eye chakra, which gave us clarity of thought and cleared any mental blockages we had. We felt so connected to this truly spiritual place.

After we had finished, the shaman took us on to the next initiation: a walk along the Serpent Path. However, we were not prepared for the sight before us, as the path was quite narrow, with a sheer drop a long way down on either side. I started to wonder if I could walk along this path that frightened the life out of me, so I started off cautiously, ahead of the others. Some were afraid and refused to move, but the shaman eventually convinced everyone to walk it, as it was part of the initiation ceremony. I turned back to see if my friend was behind me, but all I could see was that she had turned around to join the group beyond the path.

I suddenly became aware that I was alone on the Serpent Path. Gripped with fear, I was unable to move. While I was thinking I should turn back too, a man suddenly appeared by my side, and with a deep voice, he ordered me, '*Walk it!*' His powerful words seemed to break the spell of fear that had consumed me, and I did what he ordered me to do. Taking one tiny step after another, I began to walk, praying for Archangel Michael to protect me. Halfway along, a sense of calmness surrounded me and I found the strength to walk to the end of the Serpent Path. The ordeal, however, wasn't over. A huge drop to the ground awaited me at the end, and the only way down appeared to be to sit down and slide down. I've gone this far, I thought, I might as well go all the way, as there was no way I was walking back. I sat down and began to slide. When I got to the ground, a huge brown hare quickly crossed in front of me. I had never seen a hare that large before and saw its appearance as a sign of good luck. When I look back on this particular experience, I can see that the symbolism of the hare gave me a greater understanding of the direction my life would take. It taught me to trust my intuition because anything is possible when we believe.

It was a while before the rest of the group finally caught up with me. I told my friend about the man who came out of nowhere and ordered me to walk the Serpent Path. It must have been one of the shaman guides, I told her. "No, Susie, the two guides were with us the whole time," she explained. I was surprised to hear this and then it occurred to me that perhaps he was an Earth Angel?

Sometimes the answers don't always come the way you expect them to, but with faith and belief, you can see miracles come your way.

After that challenging walk and the sacred initiation of the Serpent Path, the shaman took us to an area where there was a very steep mountain drop, the place where he performs the condor bird initiation. "I'm going to hold you all around your waists and you are going to fly like a condor bird one at a time," he told us. I was not convinced. In spite of the success I had on the Serpent Path, I could picture myself falling down the mountainside with my screams echoing for miles around.

When I finally came out of my state of panic, I watched as one of the women walked to the edge and without hesitation, stretched out her arms like wings, while the shaman held her around the waist. I thought, 'OK, if she can do it, I can too.' The initiation of the Serpent Path and seeing the hare made me realise that I was capable of anything I set my mind to do, simply because things start to happen when you start to believe. Putting my trust in the shaman, I stepped forward to the edge of the cliff to receive the blessing of the condor bird and began to feel as free as a bird, my soul flying high in the open sky. I felt no fear while I stood on the edge of the cliff, and I breathed in the fresh mountain air as the wind caressed my face; I felt alive.

After the final initiation, the shaman was pleased with all of us. We had received all three initiations of the condor bird, the puma and the serpent and to round it off, the shaman lit a fire and then conducted an Andean *despacho* sacred prayer offering. We were then asked to write a few words on a piece of paper that we threw into the fire. This ceremony was to rid ourselves of bad memories from the past. The shaman then told us that any shape that appears to us in the flames is missing within us. I saw a heart, so I thought it must reflect the sadness of missing my beloved mother at such a young age. He then told us that when all the ashes were burnt, the symbolism of what we saw goes back into the protecting spirit of Mother Earth. Then he blessed us on our foreheads and prayed in the Peruvian language.

Me receiving the condor bird initiation

I finally understood the impact these initiations had on me as I reflected on Incan mythology and what we can all learn from their wisdom: The puma symbolised strength, intelligence, wisdom and patience, and was also the symbol of life on planet Earth. The serpent represented the underworld, but not in the way other cultures think of this as hell and a place for eternal punishment. The underworld symbolised the beginning of a new life for the

Incas, and the serpent was also seen to represent wisdom and knowledge. The condor bird symbolised its connection to the divine, the earth and the sky, which is why it was very sacred to the Incas. This magnificent bird was believed to carry the dead on its wings to the afterlife. Its large size and ability to travel long distances are some of the reasons why the Incas believed it to be the messenger of the heavens. These are qualities that we can all strive for in our lives.

Enlightenment is governed by initiations, ceremonies and blessings, all of which we received during this mystical and magical journey in Peru. It was very special, as I felt spiritually reconnected with Mother Earth. I found this journey to be a divinely guided process of awakening and of stepping into my true power that is aligned with the higher self. From my past experiences of listening to my higher self – a universal term used by people who feel strongly connected to spirit – I have received numerous divine messages and miracles on my path in life. This 'higher self' can be described as an awareness of your own spiritual being that is unlimited and eternal. Once you are aware of this positive divine force of life, you can create a connection with the spirit of God that opens up channels of inspiration and guides you with intuition. Your 'higher self' can teach you through insight what I like to call 'a knowing,' and sometimes can show you the path through images or a physical urge to do or not do something; we all have this ability if we are prepared to listen to the voice within and heed the message.

The next day was 22nd September – the equinox and the first day of spring in the Southern Hemisphere – and we went to explore the majestic temple of Ollantaytambo. Built in the 1400s, this large Inca fortress was also known as the Temple of the Sun with its monolithic stones, which soar above the village's cobbled streets. We then climbed up the two hundred steps to the top to get a closer look at the remains of several fountains and temples. People local to the area also like to point out an Inca face, which appears to be carved into the cliff above the valley.

While strolling through the narrow streets of Ollantaytambo village, we enjoyed the mix of colonial and old Inca architecture, and meeting the friendly locals going about their daily chores wearing traditional clothes. But it was the older women who stood out, as they collected wood and herbs and carried them home on their backs. It made us feel grateful for our many blessings in this life and we ended the day with a nice meal at a local restaurant.

Over the next few days, we continued to explore the healing altars and temples of the Sacred Valley. We visited the great salt mines of Maras, an intricate system of terraces with over three thousand salt-water ponds that have been producing the most mineral-rich pink salt in the world for more than five hundred years. It gave us a newfound sense of respect for the salt we sprinkled on our meals every day.

Proceeding to Moray, we explored the Inca ruins known as the Moray Terraces, where our guide performed a *despacho* ceremony of giving thanks to the mother-earth-goddess, Pachamama, revered by the indigenous people of the Andes as she represents fertility, planting and the harvest of the land. The offering of coca leaves, in particular, is made to appreciate the gifts of abundance bestowed by Pachamama. Other offerings in this spiritual ceremony include native Andean seeds, fruits, grains and flowers. During the ceremony, the sacred mountain deities – earth, water, air and fire – are called upon as a symbolic way in which men and women can give back to Pachamama what they have taken from the earth. It was a profound insight into the respect for Mother Nature held by the Andean people of the region – past and present – for nothing should be taken for granted; it was humbling to witness.

The following day, we checked out of the hotel and took the train to the town of Aguas Calientes for our eventual ascent of Machu Picchu. This town has breathtaking views of the Urubamba Valley – where time stands still.

After about one hour into our journey, our guide shouted, 'Come quickly!' We all rushed to the front of the train and saw a grey, round unidentified flying object with flashing lights flying overhead. Within a few seconds, it disappeared at the speed of light before anyone could take a photo. Our Peruvian guide was not surprised and told us that some of the villagers had seen UFOs over the years, and they have also been spotted flying over Machu Picchu. It was so magical to see one.

The shaman preparing the Andean despacho sacred prayer offering

The train finally arrived at our destination and after we checked into the hotel, we explored the village of Aguas Calientes and walked straight into a beautiful parade. Everyone was dressed in a variety of colourful costumes, dancing and playing traditional music and marching through the streets, some on stilts towering over us. The sights and sounds of this day were invigorating, and it was even more special when two young Peruvian girls approached and snuggled up to me, with one holding a baby llama in her arms.

Attending the parade in Aguas Calientes

After a good night's sleep, we set out at dawn, dressed in white for the long walk with our guides up the mountain to Machu Picchu for our special sunrise ceremony. As we were walking, my mind was suddenly filled with a fleeting yet terrifying thought; I had a vision of falling off the side of the mountain, which I quickly dismissed and carried on walking slowly up the mountain. On arrival at the designated spot, we grouped ourselves into a circle and began the ceremony, during which we all received a solar initiation. We felt the sun activate our chakras one by one as it rose to greet the day. This ceremony left me feeling an intense awareness of the spirit, not just within me but the group as a whole. It was a spiritual awakening and it opened my heart in many ways. After the ceremony, we sat and meditated; it was very emotional. I felt that this was one of the most magical moments of our journey. The beautiful energy that emanated all around felt like I was standing in the embrace of my mother and it gave me a new sense of purpose. I breathed deeply to fill my lungs with the sweet, clean air and thanked God for the good fortune I'd had to travel to Peru and experience this blessing that Machu Picchu gave me.

After such an uplifting day, I expected to sleep well that night but didn't, as I had a terrible dream. When I woke up, I felt very uneasy in the room and left quickly for breakfast. As I sat down at our table, a young boy said, "I had a funny dream this morning, I saw a man at the end of my bed and he had chains on like a prisoner." His mother turned around and said, "You and your dreams!" I said nothing, as I did not wish to alarm the boy, his mother, or the other people at the table, but I also had the same vision that morning, only a lot worse. I could actually hear the anguished cries and screams of men in chains, probably being tortured.

Dispelling all bad thoughts, we left the hotel and returned to Machu Picchu for another day of sightseeing and meditation. While exploring this ancient city, we felt the aura of mystery surrounding it, which seemed to affect a different chakra[11] as we walked from one spot to another. And then we were taken to the place we had all been waiting for: the Guard House, a building used by soldiers who guarded the two main entrances to Machu Picchu. Known as Huayna, we had a spectacular panoramic view of this ancient city due to its commanding high position in the south of the citadel; it was a joy to behold.

---

[11] It is generally believed that the seven chakra points on the body act as a pathway between the physical and spiritual worlds, to keep your life energy (*qi*) in balance as it journeys to the soul.

Our trip was coming to an end, and during our final dinner with the group, a few people began talking about the strange image of a man in chains they kept seeing roaming around their rooms and hallways at night. They all thought it was a figment of their imagination.

As a waitress approached our table, my friend asked her if the hotel was haunted. "Well, I have to be honest, this hotel was built on the grounds of a prison," the waitress replied. My friend continued, "My roommate had a vision about being in a prison and seeing people tortured with chains on their hands and feet." The waitress did not respond and busied herself clearing the table and quickly left. There was an uneasy feeling in the air and I kept reminding myself that we had just one more night in this hotel. 'We can do that,' I told myself, particularly now that we had been blessed and received the sacred initiations from the shaman. Later that day, I sent Reiki universal life force energy to those lost souls wandering the corridors of the hotel and hoped that they would find peace on the wings of the condor bird to deliver them to the afterlife.

The following day, we flew back to Lima with the group and said our goodbyes over a farewell dinner. It was a blessing to have shared this wonderful experience in Peru with a group of people from all over the world. I did not want to leave the 'Old Mountain' – Machu Picchu – the symbol of the Incan Empire. This mysteriously beautiful place was an uplifting experience for me. I will never forget and cherish these memories as my life's dream had been fulfilled in ways I could not have imagined. I was spiritually enriched in preparation for the next journey, destination unknown, for now.

Chapter 5

EGYPT

AND MY SOUL QUEST JOURNEY

IN JANUARY 2009, MY FRIENDS and I decided to join an international 'soul quest' journey to Egypt, organised by Patricia Cori. It was going to be a unique journey as Patricia had permission to enter the King's Chamber of the Great Pyramid to perform spiritual blessings and initiations.

As soon as we arrived at the great Temple of Luxor, which is built like a human body, we moved deeper into the temple, towards the head, where the inner sanctuary is located. A walk through this temple brings an awareness of your own body that evokes images of radiant health. As I focused on physical healing, I could feel a tingling sensation throughout my body. A sense of 'awakening' consumed me as if I had just woken up from a deep sleep. This awakening activates divinity codes and turns on your inner light. With this deeper awareness, we ventured into the world's largest temple complex: Karnak, a very sacred place.

Within this complex is a small chapel dedicated to one of the most important goddesses of ancient Egypt - Sekhmet[12] - the warrior goddess and also the goddess of healing. Depicted as a lioness, she was seen as the protector of the pharaohs and led them in warfare. Her name invoked fear and awe amongst the ancient Egyptians – it still does today, as she was commonly referred to, past and present, as 'Mistress of Dread' and 'Before whom Evil Trembles.' However, we were there to honour this great goddess and to receive the blessing of courage to be our true selves. With a heightened sense of

---

[12] https://egyptianmuseum.org/deities-sekhmet

courage, we set off from Luxor to Abydos the next day to tour the Temple of Seti the First. Abydos is one of the oldest, most sacred cities of ancient Egypt, dedicated to Osiris, the god of the underworld, resurrection and paradise. The mysterious Osirion Temple is connected to the waters of the Nile and behind the Temple of Seti the First. It is one of the foremost healing places on the planet, yet its original purpose is still unknown. This mysterious place is linked to healing in modern times through the story of Dorothy Eady (1904 –1981), a British antiques caretaker and folklorist who was also the keeper of the Abydos Temple of Seti the First, and draughtswoman for the Department of Egyptian Antiquities. She is remembered for her considerable historical research at Abydos and for her ability to heal people who came to be immersed in the healing waters of the Osirion Temple. Most of all, she is remembered for her detailed past life experiences in ancient Egypt as a priestess who had a relationship with Seti the First.[13]

As we were walking along, I mentioned to Manar, our Egyptian guide, the pain I was having in my knees. Right at that moment, we happened to pass by the Osirion Temple and Manar discreetly took me by the hand and led me away from the group to this special place. She thought the healing water might help me. On entering the temple, I saw a bat and froze; I don't like bats! But the blessing from Sekhmet began to take effect and I quickly overcame my fear as we stepped into the sacred healing water. I felt a hot, tingling sensation reverberate from my feet up to my thighs. When we left the temple to rejoin the group, I felt like I was floating on air and the pain had gone from my knees. I was healed.

It was a blessing for me to be able to go to the Osirion Temple and walk in the footsteps of many who have sought out its healing powers for millennia. It was a wonderful experience; my soul was full.

---

[13] https://en.wikipedia.org/wiki/Dorothy_Eady

The next day, we went to Luxor and made a sunrise pilgrimage to Deir El Bahari, the funerary temple of the powerful female pharaoh, Hatshepsut. We also visited the Necropolis of Thebes on the west bank of the Nile, where the Valley of the Kings is located, which holds the pharaohs' tombs that are inscribed with sacred transformative texts. I was humbled by the knowledge all around.

We left Luxor and set sail for the Temple of Edfu, dedicated to Horus, a falcon-headed god. This is a beautifully preserved temple and as you approach the complex, you become aware of its enormous dimensions, with a vast courtyard, a forest of towering columns and high ceilings; it was awe-inspiring. The temple's side chambers show the complexity of ancient rites. Horus is associated with higher vision and clarity, and the symbol of the eye of Horus greatly relates to his myth and healing power. In this temple, one can seek to balance the lunar and solar energies inside of us and awaken our intuition to experience a higher perspective.

A short boat trip further up the Nile led us to the unique 'double' temple site of Kom Ombo, only a ten-minute walk from the dock. As this temple is dedicated to two gods, all the chambers within have been duplicated in exact proportions along the central axis of the building: the southern part of the temple is dedicated to Sobek, the crocodile god of strength, fortitude, fertility, and rebirth; and the northern half to Horus, also known as the falcon god of the sky and kingship. [14] The duality of the light/dark, yin/yang and conscious/unconscious energies became apparent and even more powerful as we approached the Seat of Neutrality, located on the exact centerline between the two parts of the temple.

After Kom Ombo, we sailed on to an island to visit the Temple of Philae, which is dedicated to Isis, the goddess of protection, motherhood and rebirth. After receiving a blessing at her beautiful temple site, I felt cleansed and

---

[14] https://en.wikipedia.org/wiki/Temple_of_Kom_Ombo

peaceful. We were sad to leave the island, but enjoyed the boat cruise back to Luxor, taking in the sights of village life along the way.

On our last day in Cairo, we had permission for a private visit inside the Great Pyramid early that morning at 4 am, which culminated in an initiation in the King's Chamber. When we arrived, Patricia asked us all, one by one, to lie down on the granite sarcophagus (tomb) for her to give us the activation of the throat, third eye, and crown chakras. This process opens up the throat chakra's communication channels enhancing the ability to listen, to be heard, and to have your needs met. A balanced throat chakra helps to set us free from fear, judgement or the need for approval from others. The third eye chakra, also known as the 'ajna' that is believed to be connected to the pineal gland, opens up your awareness of self and spiritual communication, improves concentration, and strengthens intuition. When the crown chakra is activated, it will connect you to spirit as well as your senses of universal consciousness, wisdom, unity and self-knowledge. This process is designed to rid the mind/body/soul of negative emotions, such as anger, resentment or worry.

After the initiation, we all joined hands in a circle and began to sing. Some of us heard angelic chanting that appeared to come from higher realms, a high-pitched melody engulfing us in sound that gave me instant goose bumps. It was the most beautiful, mystical music that filled the whole of the King's Chamber. The energy made me feel like I was floating on air and at peace. After the ceremony, we stayed there for a half hour, bathing in this beautiful energy. We felt so uplifted we hugged each other and walked towards 'the darkest of the darkest' – a subterranean tunnel that descended under the pyramid. Some of the group refused to go. Putting my fear behind me, I agreed to venture into the unknown, along with Salma and Shireen. Patricia advised us that whoever goes through this tunnel will conquer their fears. I approached the passageway and felt very uneasy, uncertain whether or not I should proceed, when the blessing of Sekhmet's courage rose up to put those thoughts behind me.

I bent down onto my hands and knees and began to crawl through the tunnel. Halfway through, I was overcome by claustrophobia and began to sweat, thinking, 'Is this ever going to end?' I had no choice; I had to keep going.

The end finally appeared and we were able to stand up straight with a tremendous sense of relief until Patricia shouted, "Light's going off!" We found ourselves wrapped in complete darkness. It was a profound symbol to help us recognise our inner strength, but we were all apprehensive about what would come next. We sat and silently meditated with our eyes open in the pitch darkness. Suddenly, I saw a magnificent sight as sparkling white crystals fell from above, showering us with positive, pure, white energy. I felt physically attuned to a higher dimension as this beautiful crystal energy embraced my soul.

This uplifting moment was brought to a close when our guide put the lights back on, although the positive energy we took from this experience remained with us for a few days longer. It was time to return and crawl back on our hands and knees. The fear I had felt going down this dark and foreboding tunnel seemed to have disappeared on our way back. As we emerged from 'the darkest of the darkest', we were met enthusiastically by the rest of the group who had remained behind, content to congratulate us on our courage. Patricia was right; we had conquered our fears.

How the Great Pyramid of King Khufu (Cheops in Greek) was built remains a mystery. As I stood in awe and wonderment, gazing up at its immense size and creative genius, I could not help but wonder how the ancient Egyptians managed to build such a structure and from where they got their knowledge. Surely, it proved that the Great Pyramid encodes the dimensions of our planet? Were the ancient Egyptians in contact with other life forms and exchanged knowledge that helped them to construct such a great and inspiring monument?

I doubt we will ever know. As we walked over to admire the Sphinx, the guardian of the pyramids, I could feel the energy of the spirits protecting its secrets.

Our visit to Egypt was filled with wondrous sights, divine love, grace and special blessings, and it was sadly coming to an end. Each visit, through the memories of eras long passed, left me with a depth of knowledge and spiritual enlightenment that made every step a meaningful and uplifting experience. It gave me a greater understanding of my being, which helped me to become more spiritual in my daily life. It was magical to go on this soul-quest journey to one of the Seven Wonders of the Ancient World. I hope to return one day.

Chapter 6

CHURCH OF SAINT GEORGE
SALT, IN NORTHERN JORDAN

THE CITY OF SALT IN northern Jordan has been attracting settlers to its fertile hills for the last three thousand years. Despite its long history, very little remains from its ancient past, except for the walls of an old Ammonite castle and the Church of Saint George nestled amongst the houses in the centre of the old city. According to oral history, the locals first built this church as a shrine dedicated to Saint George (known in Arabic as *Al Khader*) in 1682 after he appeared before a mute shepherd resting in a cave around which the church is built. It is said that Saint George gave the shepherd the power of speech, the first of many miracles that happened on this site. Although time and modernisation have reduced the size of the cave to a small grotto within the expanded church building, this site is revered and visited by people of all faiths and all nationalities. Today, Salt is now a thriving multi-religious city with churches and mosques, and it is easy to see why the locals view it as blessed.

This church is very special, not only because of the story of its existence but also because of the many miraculous healings that have occurred here over the years, including giving the blind the power to see. It is probably the only place in Jordan where Christians and Muslims pray together, which is beautiful to witness as the world is trying to pull everybody apart. UNESCO recognised this important aspect of the social and religious harmony of the city when it added the City of Salt, "the city of tolerance and civilised hospitality," to the 2021 World Heritage List.[15]

I visit this church regularly as the energy within its ancient walls feeds my soul and uplifts my spirit. However, one day in 2009, I went there for a specific reason: to fulfil a vision I had when Jesus appeared to me in a dream and told me to go to the Church of Saint George. He also said to me that I would see his face in the cave. So I asked my group of friends if they would like to visit the church with me and they all agreed.

St George's Church, Salt

When we arrived, I went directly to the cave, walked up the three steps and knelt to pray. After a long while, I began to question the dream I had that morning, as no sign had appeared. Meanwhile, my friends were listening to the

---

[15] (https://whc.unesco.org/en/list/689)

story of a recent miracle that was being told to them by the caretaker of the church. He explained how one evening, some of the neighbours saw all the lights on inside the church and heard a noisy commotion coming from inside the church building. They also heard the sounds of horses' hooves. They were so concerned that they phoned the police. When they came to inspect the church, they found nobody there. However, what they did find were marks on the walls of the cave, as if they had been cut with a sharp blade – possibly sword cuttings from Saint George's sword – and also what appeared to be an image of Jesus' face cut into the stone of the cave wall, along with a large footprint of a man and the hoof prints of horses left in the hard cement floor. These miraculous happenings increased the number of visitors to the church, both Muslim and Christian alike. As of today, this footprint, which is believed to belong to Saint George, is protected inside a glass case.

Meanwhile, I was a little upset because I had yet to see the face of Jesus in the cave. Salma approached the caretaker and told him about my dream. He was slightly shocked and said, "She must be blessed!" The caretaker then walked over to where I was praying and pointed out to us the face of Jesus engraved on the right-hand side of the cave wall. He also pointed out the place where miraculous oil oozes from the stone, which many people use to bless themselves and their rosary beads. Upon realising what my eyes were looking at, my heart began to beat faster and tears began to pour down my face. I was so overwhelmed with emotion, as were my friends, because my dream had manifested itself. It was a blessing for us all and we felt spiritually uplifted as we gathered ourselves for the journey back to Amman. This vision was a powerful reaffirmation of the work I had accepted in this lifetime; it was truly humbling to know that I was on the right path to send love and healing to Mother Earth and its people. I now understand what God meant during my near-death experience all those years ago[16] when He told me, 'You have to go back down and spread love and light to Mother Earth.'

Since the year 2000, many people have come to Jordan to study and measure ley-lines and energy spots around the Kingdom. Overall, their findings indicate that the energy levels at the Church of St. George in Salt were some of the highest readings of all other energy spots in Jordan, comparable to those found at Baidha, near Petra in southern Jordan. I was not surprised because every time I visit this church, I feel a surge of spiritual energy and a deep, almost overwhelming connection, and I am completely at peace.

Over the next year, I felt I was being drawn closer to Jesus through visions and dreams, which then took me all over Jordan with my close friends. So our next trip took us to the place of Jesus' baptism, Bethany Beyond the Jordan on the eastern side of the River Jordan, roughly five kilometres north of the Dead Sea.

The face of Jesus carved into the wall of the grotto, St. George's Church, Salt

---

[16] Mentioned in my first book, Only Time Will Tell.

Chapter 7

THE BAPTISM SITE AND THE RIVER JORDAN

FOR ME, THE BAPTISM SITE is very sacred, not only because it is the main biblical site in Jordan but also because of the many blessings I have received here over the years. It is the place where God's voice was heard on Earth through the Holy Spirit – in the form of a white dove – who came down and rested upon Jesus at the time of his baptism. Thus began Christianity.

It was the spring of 2010, and I had an amazing vision early one morning. I saw myself on the mountain where Jesus was crucified. I was standing at the foot of Jesus' cross, which looked huge against the dark, foreboding sky, and at the bottom of the cross, I could see bold letters written in Latin on a plaque: *"In nomine Patris et Filii et Spiritus Sancti."* (In the name of the Father and of the Son and of the Holy Spirit)

In my dream, it was as though I had been transported two thousand years back in time; I was at Jesus' crucifixion. I was overwhelmed and in total disbelief that Jesus was being crucified in front of me.

Suddenly, my husband woke me up, asking, "Are you okay? You were talking in your sleep and very distressed," he said. I then realised that I had been dreaming but could not get that image out of my mind. When I went into the kitchen to make breakfast I found a tiny plastic red cross on my kitchen counter and had no idea where it came from. I showed my husband and said, "Look Amin, do you know where this came from?" He shrugged his shoulders, and said, "Susie, that's funny because you dreamt about Jesus on the cross this morning."

Without thinking, I put it to one side and went to pull up the blinds in the lounge. As I looked up at the sky, I saw a perfectly formed cloud in the shape of a cross. 'That's funny, that's the second cross I have seen today.' I thought nothing of it again and called Amin into the kitchen for breakfast. Just as I left the lounge, I noticed a leaf had fallen from the plant and as I went to pick it up, I was surprised to see that the leaf was in the shape of a cross. What was the meaning of seeing three crosses? And I recalled the words of my Reiki Master, Aila, who always told me to call my friend Shirley if I had any questions, as she would know how to explain things. So I called Shirley and told her about my dream and the three crosses I had found that morning. She went quiet. "Susie, what day is it today?" I replied, "21st, which, when added together is 3, and the third month, March, is also 3, and the year 2010, when added across is also 3." She paused and then said, "It's 3-3-3, which refers to the ascended masters, including Jesus, the Virgin Mary, Melchizedek, Saint Germain, Archangel Michael, Kuthumi and many more."

I pondered on this knowledge for a while, and then my higher self told me to go to church. I phoned a friend and asked her if she would take me. "Of course, Susie, my pleasure," she said. Something told me to dress all in white that day. When we arrived, the church was packed and there was not one empty seat downstairs. It was full of mostly women from the Philippines who were singing beautiful hymns, filling the whole church with positive energy. We managed our way through the crowd to go upstairs, and to our amazement, there was not one person there, which was unusual. Sometimes the church is so full of people that the congregation spreads out onto the pavement outside. When I sat down, my eyes were drawn to a large picture on the wall; a picture of Jesus dressed all in white with his hands outstretched. I realised then how connected I am to the spirit of Jesus.

A couple of weeks later, my group of spiritual friends picked me up and we drove to the Baptism Site, located on the heavily guarded border between the Israeli-occupied West Bank of Palestine and Jordan. This is why the site only allows guided tours. When we arrived, we bought our tickets and boarded the shuttle bus to take us down to the main site. After fifteen minutes, the bus dropped us off and our guide escorted us along the path that had been cut through the undergrowth of the valley to the River Jordan. After a while, I suddenly felt very unsteady on my feet and light-headed. Two friends rushed over to help and supported me as we walked along this biblical path. The energy that surged within my body was like nothing I had felt before. I knew instinctively that this was the path where Jesus had walked over two thousand years ago.

Path through the undergrowth down to the Baptism site

I was so overwhelmed with emotion that it brought me to tears. I felt deeply connected to Jesus, especially after the vision I had a few weeks before. I thanked God for giving me this wonderful sign of the three crosses and I felt incredibly blessed.

The guide brought us to the first stop where there are three churches, three caves and three baptism pools accessible by means of wooden steps, from where you can look down and see the site of Jesus' baptism. With the passing of time, the course of the River Jordan has moved eastwards, which means that the very place of Jesus' baptism is no longer at the river's edge, as it has moved inland. The guide then turned around and asked us if we would like to go to the exact place where Jesus was baptised. Despite the presence of many other people on our tour, my friends and I were the only ones he asked. It was as if he knew how important it was for all of us to go to that sacred spot. "I will give you ten minutes to pray," he said as he moved the barrier aside and walked on with the rest of the group, leaving us alone.

It had rained heavily the previous night and the place of Jesus' baptism was full of water. Tears rolled down my cheeks as I felt complete calmness surround us, as if we were at one with our biblical surroundings, connected through time and place.

Our ten minutes came to an end and we rejoined the group walking down towards the River Jordan. On arrival, you can see a small font that has been built for people to hold baptism ceremonies. Beyond the steps, you reach the waters of the River Jordan. Only eight metres away on the other side of the river, you are faced with armed Israeli guards. After a while, we began the walk back to the bus, stopping off to visit the Orthodox Church dedicated to John the Baptist where we took time to offer prayers. It was here that I bought some wooden rosary beads, which had a beautiful smell of rose essence. I thought they would be nice to hang in my healing room. But later on, you will see why I had to buy them.

Praying at the Baptism site

I believe that this journey was a sign from Jesus, who showed me clearly where He had walked and where He had been baptised. I felt I was connecting with God's love, for this is the way home.

Nothing will stop what is meant for you when you are on God's divine path, as life will open up for you along the way. It is up to us to be aware of the signs that the universe provides for us. When you reach the point of self-belief and faith that is when you will see blessings fall upon you.

Chapter 8

A BEDOUIN PREDICTION
AND MY VISIT TO CHINA

IT WAS THE SPRING OF 2014, time for the wild flowers to bloom in the desert. I longed to take another trip south but did not have the time, as I was fully booked up with appointments. One morning, when I opened the door to receive my next client, I was surprised to see a Bedouin woman with henna tattoos on her hands and face, smiling at me in the doorway, along with her friend. I sensed a strong, wise woman standing before me, probably younger than she appeared. Strange, I thought to myself, I don't usually get clients like her, but my inner voice told me that she was here to relay a message to me. The younger woman explained that she would translate, so I welcomed them into my kitchen, where I began the reading.

I had finished with my Bedouin client and started reading for her friend when I noticed that the Bedouin woman seemed to be talking to herself. "Who is she talking to?" I asked her friend. The wise old woman turned to her friend and said in Arabic, "My spirit guides are telling me that Susie lost a ring in an area near a camp in Baidha." I nearly fell off the chair as I was totally shocked to hear this. "How does she know that?" I asked. She smiled and told her friend, "My spirit guides told me to tell Susie that they had to take something from her in exchange for the power they gave her. She will understand at the right time." I sat silently absorbing what they had just told me.

I then thought back to the time I was in Baidha four years ago, when the guide took us to an area he called 'fairyland.' I remembered that he had told me the same thing. I was still upset about that incident and asked the Bedouin woman to explain what they had given me. She replied, "I can't tell you. You will know at the right time. They are also telling me you will go to China in 2017 with another girl who is spiritual like yourself, and you will see a past life in a dream. You will walk the Great Wall of China as you have work to do there. You will know exactly where to go. It's all in the divine plan and you will have work also to do somewhere else. You will be guided and you will know once you go there." This was the sign I needed to believe that a visit to China was my destiny. Sometimes the answers don't always come the way we expect.

Fast-forward to 2017, and one day in February, I received an interesting email from Donna, who wrote that something was telling her that we both had to go to China. Knowing how intuitive Donna is, I agreed and we decided to plan a trip to China in March of that year. I flew to London a few weeks before departure to make it easier to process the paperwork for our visas.

While in the UK, we went to stay with Donna's friend, Cheaya, a special person who represents God's divine energy in her work as a light-worker, an 'up-lifter' who brings joy and consciousness to people who seek her wisdom. Her home in the Cotswolds was full of her positive energy, enhanced by rare crystals of black obsidian obtained from the Egyptian desert, as well as rose quartz, amethyst and quartz crystals. It was a reflection of her sacred journey in life. I slept well that night and had a vision of the Terracotta Army. I could see the soldiers all lined up one behind the other, like a marching army, complete with horses and carriages in a darkish clay colour; then I woke up. Discussing my vision over breakfast, Donna reminded me what Robin and the Bedouin woman had told me. "You will go to China in 2017, Susie, and you will see a past life," she replied. "Ah yes, I forgot about that."

We had a wonderful time with Cheaya, who showed us around the village and took us to a quaint coffee shop. I ordered scones with raspberry jam, fresh cream and a lovely cup of brewed coffee. 'How much I miss my English scones,' I thought. We then walked to the village church and as no one was inside, we entered and began to sing. The sound of our voices echoing around this quaint church filled me with joy and I felt as if the angelic realm had joined us; it was uplifting because singing is a tool for spiritual healing. We said our good-byes the next morning and returned to Donna's house.

A few days later, Donna and I were invited for lunch at a friend's house, a short drive away in the countryside. On the way, we stopped at a lovely garden centre to buy our hostess some flowers. As we walked around admiring the beautiful plants on display, Donna suddenly called for me, "Susie, come quickly, look!" I walked over and I could not believe what I saw, as there in front of me was a statue of a terracotta soldier. The soldier's left arm was bent across his stomach and placed towards his solar plexus. It felt strange to see a statue of a terracotta soldier in the middle of the English countryside. We were both taken aback and Donna thought it was a sign. "You will probably know when we arrive in China," she said. I knew she was right.

At the garden centre in Kent, I got my sign

A couple of days later, we landed in Shanghai and met up with the rest of our tour group at the hotel. We enjoyed a quick evening dinner to get to know our fellow travellers who had come from all over the world, and retired early to bed. We had decided to join a tour group for our safety, as we felt it wasn't a good idea to travel to China on our own.

The highlight of our first tour was a visit to the Jade Buddha Temple, one of the most famous temples in Shanghai. This temple provided a peaceful retreat from the hustle and bustle all around, and we retired to the hotel that evening feeling content.

The next day we travelled to the village of Zhou Zhuang, often referred to as the number one water village in China because of its interconnected waterways and beautiful environment. Donna and I felt so at peace while walking around its scenic landscaped gardens while admiring the modest architecture of its traditional homes that were built during the Ming and Qing dynasties. They have been well preserved for over 900 years and it was a striking contrast to the architecture of the Shanghai Bund.

That evening, a dinner was planned on a riverboat cruise. Before joining the rest of the group, Donna and I wandered around, admiring the scenery. Just as I was about to take a photo of the beautiful quayside, I fell to the ground, hard on my knees and left shoulder, as if someone had pushed me from behind. I looked around, but there was no one there. The only thing visible was my camera smashed on the floor. Shocked and upset, I could not stop crying, and the tour guide rushed over to comfort me. "I am not going to any hospital," I told him between sobs. Donna came running up to me, "Susie, are you okay? I didn't even hear or see you fall," she cried with a concerned look on her face. "I was pushed, Donna, I know the difference between a push and a fall." I then had a strong feeling that something was trying to stop me from the mission I was meant to do. This feeling of being physically and mentally attacked is best described as a 'psychic attack'— often associated with forces of darkness. In this case, I believe that this 'push' was on such a negative level; its aim was to stop the mission I came to do on the Great Wall of China. At that point, I was still unsure of the exact nature of my mission.

Determined to carry on, we struggled onto the boat and headed to the bathroom, where Donna put cold water on my knees to stop the bleeding. It was only the second day of our trip and I was already injured. I sat in a state of shock and all I could think of was my bed. I just wanted to curl up and sleep. I don't remember much else from that evening.

When we returned to the hotel, my left shoulder was giving me a lot of pain; a terrible excruciating, throbbing pain, and I could barely walk through the lobby. I felt it was serious, but more troublesome was the fact that I began to feel my determination to go on was fading, despite the inner strength within my being.

"Who gave you the ice to put on my knees, it felt so good and soothing?" I asked Donna. "What ice?" she replied and explained that it was just water from the tap. "I swear it was ice!"

That night, before I slept, I sent out Reiki universal energy to heal myself if it was my divine right to continue my mission. I needed a miracle; 'only time will tell,' I thought.

When I woke up the next morning, I was afraid to pull the blankets down to check how bad my knees were. I summoned up the courage to get out of bed and realised I could walk without pain, and there wasn't even a scratch or bruise to be seen on either knee. Donna could not believe what she was seeing either. "Susie, I didn't want to tell you, but your knee had popped out to the side of your leg and so I just pushed it back in place. I was very worried about you. But now, what a miracle I am seeing that you can walk after that bad fall. This is the sign you asked for. But what about your shoulder?" Donna asked. "I can manage with my left arm and shoulder despite the pain, I can use a scarf to make a sling. I feel that I have dislocated it." I wasn't going to give in to the forces of darkness or spoil my trip, so I took some strong painkillers; at least I could walk without problems. I had received the sign I had asked for and I thanked God for the blessing.

Early the next day, we took a flight to Xian. Upon arrival, we checked into our hotel. We were eager to get on the coach to visit the Terracotta Army, quite possibly, the greatest archaeological discovery of the twentieth century.

When we arrived, we walked to the museum and went straight to Pit One, the most famous pit, where one had a view of the Terracotta Army, whose statues of warriors were displayed in military formation. We squeezed through the crowds to the left of the main entrance and slowly pushed our way to the front barrier. Once there, we gazed out on row after row of clay warriors crafted more than two thousand years ago to guard China's first emperor, Qin Shi Huang (259-210 BC), in the afterlife.[17] Despite being a great emperor who is famous for unifying China after centuries of division, he is also known as an oppressive ruler during his short but significant dynasty.

We learnt that it took nearly 700,000 forced labourers and craftsmen nearly thirty-eight years to build the emperor's vast burial complex during his lifetime, a necropolis estimated to cover an area of between 55 and 98 sq. km.

Researchers also discovered that the thousands of people who worked on the mausoleum project were either killed or buried alive in the burial pits around the emperor's tomb. This brutal measure was taken to keep the secrets of the Terracotta Army – a replica of the army of Qin – from being discovered. For millennia, the tomb of China's first emperor, guarded by eight thousand terracotta soldiers and archers, complete with weaponry, jade objects and horses leading bronze chariots, were left undiscovered until 1974, when they were unearthed by local farmers. [18]

---

[17] www.chinahighlights.com
[18] www.chinahighlights.com

As I stood looking down at the pit, essentially still an archaeological dig, I felt overwhelmed. The soldiers in the first few rows looked like they were standing at attention, facing the incoming crowd. They were amazingly life-like, all with different facial features, hairstyles and armour, and it felt as if they could simply wake up and start marching along, as the real army would have done over two thousand years before.

Me and Donna (right) at Pit 1 of the museum of the Terracotta Army

I felt frozen in time and overcome with a sense of *déjà vu*, which caused all my hair to stand up on end because this was exactly the vision I saw in my dream in England; it was amazing to see. It was also the sign that meant I was supposed to be here, in China, to do the work that God sent me to do.

Despite the crowds, Donna and I split up to find a quiet space, as we knew what we had to do: release the lost souls that had been trapped within this monumental burial complex. After we had finished our work, we met up again and Donna explained her part of our spiritual work. She had visualised floating particles of light going upwards as she sent out a prayer for the lost souls. I felt that all those particles were going straight through my body upwards to heaven; it was so powerful that my heart was racing. "That's what I prayed for Susie, and you felt it!" Another feeling of *déjà vu* overcame me; it was as if I was one of them. I felt so exhausted after this spiritual experience that tears began to roll down my face, almost as if these pure, tiny drops of water were anointing me with God's grace. Within a few moments, exhaustion turned to strength and we saw clearly the purpose of our mission.

We gathered ourselves and rejoined the group at the Museum gift shop. I was surprised at how well I was doing, as my left arm was still in a sling, which is probably why the sales girl behind the counter suddenly handed me a statue of a terracotta soldier with his left arm bent towards his solar plexus. She then told me these were the archers and that they were the most spiritual of the Terracotta Army. "Take it, take it, it's for you! A gift," she said. I felt she knew what I had come to do.

I then realised the meaning of the statue she gave me. I saw myself through this terracotta archer, as my left hand was in a sling, with my arm bent and facing my solar plexus, just like the terracotta soldier statue I saw in the garden centre in England. For the sales girl to gift me this statue was a sign that I was an archer in the Qin Army in a past life. It also confirmed that my mission with the Terracotta Army had been completed

We flew to Beijing, and over the next few days, we immersed ourselves in imperial Chinese history, touring the Forbidden City, the Temple of Heaven, and the Summer Palace while also enjoying a visit to a pearl market and a traditional medicine centre. Finally, we went through the ancient north gate to Tiananmen Square with its many monuments testifying to Chairman Mao Zedong's communist influence on China's modern history. The guide advised us to be silent as we walked around the square, and never to mention the massacre that took place there in 1989. If the police heard anyone talking about it, "one would be put in prison," we were told. All I felt there was an air of sadness, so Donna and I sent out Reiki universal energy all around the square.

On the last day of our tour, we travelled by bus early in the morning to the Great Wall of China, which in Chinese means 'The Long Wall of 10,000 Miles,' arriving before the crowds. After a short hike, we were rewarded with marvellous views of this ancient Wall as it stretched for miles through the surrounding countryside. Our tour guide gave us two hours to explore the Wall on our own and when finished, we were instructed to meet at the gift shop at the entrance. To our relief, everyone went off to explore and Donna and I were left alone, as it was meant to be. I could not help thinking about the Bedouin woman who came to see me a few years ago. Her prediction was right, as I was standing on the Great Wall of China in 2017! I suddenly realised what she meant when she told me, "You will go somewhere else too and will know what to do." It was to the Terracotta Army.

Fortunately, we did not have far to walk, as a cable car was parked nearby as if it was waiting to take us where we needed to go. We were all alone with no other tourists, so we climbed in and enjoyed the ride with magnificent views of the Wall down below. It was also a relief to sit down in comfort, as my shoulder was giving me some pain.

From the cable car, we took in the historic landscape covered in so many shades of green; we were lucky as the weather was kind to us that day. "Can you imagine how many people died building the Great Wall of China?" I said to Donna. There is no doubt that the construction of the various sections of the Wall caused untold human suffering among the labour force,[19] which was made up largely of soldiers, particularly during Emperor Qin Shi Huang's dynasty. Common people and convicts were also conscripted into the construction project, and it is said that many hundreds of thousands of people died during the Wall's many periods of construction.

We finally got to our destination as the cable car came to a complete stop. We got out, walked along the wall, which was hard going, and arrived at a sentry post. We went inside and blessed all the walls. Then, my higher self told me to go further up, so we took the stairs inside the sentry post to the top. "Let me go behind you so you don't fall or hurt the other arm," said Donna. We both knew that this was the place where we had to do our work.

Along the Great Wall of China; the sanctuary post in the background

---

[19] https://www.travelchinaguide.com/china_great_wall/facts/who-built.htm#1

We were completely alone as we sent out a blessing of Reiki universal life force energy to release the lost souls who had died during the construction of the Wall. During the ceremony, a lovely young woman with blue eyes appeared out of nowhere. She had an angelic smile and carried a large radio that was playing the most beautiful and calming music; as if the angels were giving us the strength and guidance we needed to do our work.

Leaving the sentry post, we summoned all our energy to trek back down the Wall when Donna told me that she had asked for a sign to show her that the work we had done that day was accepted and confirmed. She needed to know that we had accomplished our mission. As we continued down the Wall, Donna stopped and pointed in the distance, "Look, Susie, there's something red climbing up the side of the mountain over there, and it's coming towards us."

As we stood there, the red image came into view; it was a man dressed as a warrior in ancient costume, complete with a sword and a black and gold helmet. He came up to us and smiled, and we smiled back. Then, much to our surprise, a tourist appeared and took a picture of us all. The presence of these two men showed us that symbolically we had completed our mission. Donna definitely got her sign that we considered a blessing from above.

Despite the blessings we had just received and the mission we had carried out, the energy I felt on the Wall was unnerving. Donna felt it too. And suddenly, it registered, and I finally understood what I had been given in the 'fairyland' area of Baidha in southern Jordan, where my ring was taken all those years ago: it was pure energy to give me the strength I needed to help release all the lost souls who should not have been buried for millennia around the Great Wall. It was a matter of divine timing.

After a challenging walk down, we arrived at our meeting point before everyone else, so we sat on a bench to drink our orange juice. Suddenly, I noticed a large beetle next to my pink shoes staring up at me with its big eyes.

"He must like my pink shoes," I joked. I got up and walked slowly away and the beetle seemed to follow me. I said to Donna, "See if he follows you." And sure enough, he did. I knew then that it wasn't my pink shoes attracting him. I believe that insects of every kind and all animals have the intelligence to understand us, especially as they are all God's creatures. I sat back down and talked to the beetle. "Hello," I said, "what do you want?" and gave him some of my orange juice on the floor, but he certainly wasn't thirsty. The beetle was a sandy light grey colour, similar to the colour of the terracotta warriors. With his big eyes looking up at me, my higher self was telling me he was from the underworld. Donna felt it was strange too. Finally, as if he understood what we were thinking, the beetle turned around and walked off.

The red warrior – Donna got her sign!

A while later, as soon as everyone had regrouped, we boarded the bus for our long trip back to the hotel. About half an hour into our journey, I took my arm out of the scarf sling to put my hand on the back of the chair to stretch out the muscles. I was amazed at how well I was coping with my shoulder injury; that was a miracle in itself.

Looking out of the window at the high-rise buildings flashing past me, I felt compassion for the Chinese people seeing how they lived in mile upon mile of cramped apartment buildings, with washing hanging out of every window. 'God bless them all,' that's all I could think.

All of a sudden, I felt something crawling on my left hand. When I looked down, I was surprised to see it was the same beetle I had befriended at the entrance to the Great Wall of China. 'How can this be?' I wondered as we both saw the beetle walk off into the distance about forty-five minutes before we boarded the bus. I looked at my hand as the beetle looked up at me and although I wasn't afraid initially, a sense of fear overcame me at the thought of how he ended up on my hand. Donna could not believe her eyes either. I whispered in her ear, "Don't kill him." She grabbed a tissue, carefully caught the beetle and called out to the driver to stop the bus. He parked the bus and opened the door while Donna carefully put the beetle onto the grass edge of the pavement. "Are you frightened of beetles, love?" said someone from the group. "Yes, I am scared of all creepy-crawly things," I lied; none of the tourists had any idea what we had done on the Great Wall and what I truly felt about this beetle, and I planned to keep it that way.

Our China trip came to an end and we both knew and felt that we had accomplished our mission. We arrived in England with three days left of my holiday. Donna and I were both exhausted, not only from the exertion of using so much life force energy but also from travelling around China, as every day for a week our programme began at seven in the morning and ended at nine in the evening, never returning once to the hotel for a change of clothes or a shower for the evening entertainment. We never did get to use the lovely eveningwear we had brought with us. We could not eat much either, as we were put off by the smell of the food. We lived on eggs, rice and ice cream. At least I lost weight!

The next day, Rania Kurdi, a friend of ours from Amman and a well-known actress who lives between Jordan and England, joined us for a sumptuous lunch, and afterwards, we decided to walk it off in a beautiful park near Donna's house. I told Rania of my plans to turn my first book, *Only Time Will Tell*, into an audio version but that I did not have a clue how to do it. Rania said, "Don't worry, Susie, I will do it for you."

When I returned to Jordan, my energy levels hit rock bottom and I knew my immune system was down, so I stayed in bed for nearly a week while my lovely husband, Amin, took care of me. I was not surprised though, as the mission I had just accomplished required a high level of energy and it left me completely drained.

A week later, after regaining my strength, I phoned Shirley and told her about my trip in the hope that she could shed some light on the beetle incident. Shirley is excellent at interpreting spiritual situations, and she immediately sensed that the beetle had an innocent curiosity as to who had cleansed the underworld. She continued to explain that the work we had done amounted to two things: the cleansing of the underworld where the lost souls had been trapped – as they should not have been there to begin with – and the releasing of those lost souls.

The meaning of the beetle's appearance, not once but twice, was an affirmation of my mission; it was to deliver a simple, high-level message from the universe: 'thank you,' the beetle was telling me.

Chapter 9

WADI RUM, SOUTHERN JORDAN

LOCATED IN THE SOUTH OF JORDAN is our famous 'Valley of the Moon' – Wadi Rum – a vast wilderness of semi-arid desert that is now a protected area. It is known for its spectacular sand dunes, narrow canyons and dramatic, colourful, mountainous rock formations – a haven for trekkers, tourists, photographers and filmmakers. It is also a place to stargaze and it speaks to my soul.

And so it was, in August 2018, that Donna was in town. She popped over for coffee one morning and we both felt that we needed to connect with the desert while she was in Jordan, so we decided to visit Wadi Rum after our trip to Mount Nebo.

My friends and I like to go on spiritual trips in nature at least once a month, especially when the weather is mild in the spring – when Jordan is so green and all the lovely wild flowers are in full bloom. However, we were still in the hot summer month of August but decided to go to Mount Nebo and visit the churches of Madaba, a short drive outside of Amman.

After our visit, we went to a souvenir shop. As we entered, I was drawn to the silver jewellery counter, where this beautiful pear-shaped ring seemed to be staring up at me, and I could not resist buying it. I was told it was a blue goldstone gem, which was significant as this stone has healing properties. Its indigo-blue colour appeared to shimmer within the stone and it reminded me of the night skies of Wadi Rum. Little did I know that Donna had bought exactly the same ring.

This was no coincidence, as we were going to Wadi Rum in a couple of days. Donna then told me about a dream she had that night about Wadi Rum. "I saw a red carpet and red rose petals all the way on our trip. We have to take a bottle of red wine with us, as it's part of the ceremony," Donna said. She felt that her dream was a sign that symbolically meant the whole trip would go smoothly, even though the temperature in the desert would be over forty degrees. We felt guided to do spiritual work in the desert, not only to connect with Christ consciousness[20] and our higher selves but also to spread love, light and peace to the world. I knew that those rings were another sign showing us the way forward.

On the day before departure, Donna rang me to say that she did not have the time to buy the wine. I told her not to worry and to leave it up to the universe. Shortly after that, a client arrived for her consultation, and she was carrying a bottle of red wine. "Susie, I hope you don't mind, but something told me to give this to you." I smiled at her as I knew that the universe had given me my sign, even though no one had ever given me a bottle of wine in the forty years of my work. All I could say was, "thank you." As soon as the client left, I rang Donna and told her that we had our bottle of wine. "Talk about synchronicity, Susie." When we make sacred trips, we cannot always remember why we go and what we are to do, as we are guided and shown the way.

We departed for Wadi Rum the following day, 11th August, which was perfect timing because the best time of year for stargazing is between 9th and 13th August; we were bound to see a lot of magical shooting stars. As we settled into our tent at Captain's Desert Camp, I mentioned to Donna that I was guided to bring along meditation music dedicated to the goddess Isis, known throughout the ancient world for fertility and magical healing of the sick, amongst many other powers. As the sun set over the glorious landscape, we

---

[20] For further information on Christ consciousness, please visit:
https://www.yogapedia.com/definition/5806/christ-consciousness

stepped outside to explore. The camp seemed empty, as it was the hottest month of the season. We did not mind, as we were guided to this magical place. We ran into the only other guests at the camp, a couple from Japan. They joined us for dinner and we spent an enjoyable evening chatting about Jordan.

After dinner, we asked the manager to show us the best place to meditate. He guided us to a very quiet spot and kindly brought us two chairs with a table. We glanced up at the night sky and noticed how cloudy it was; not a star to be seen. "Don't worry, Susie, we will see them soon, when the clouds pass." Don't worry? I thought to myself rather glumly, as I was so disappointed. I am sure Donna was too, but she did not say a word. I played the soothing Isis music and we both meditated for a while before we retired for the night.

At about 1:30 am, a very loud tapping at the window woke me up. I looked over at Donna and she was fast asleep, but I could not contain myself as I was so afraid and shouted, "Donna wake up, someone tapped at the window, did you not hear it?" It took a while for Donna to wake up, but when she realised what I was saying, she leapt out of bed and pointed at the window, "Look, Susie, look at the sky, they woke us up to see the view!" I peered out of the window and the whole sky looked magnificent! We were so excited and went outside. We sat on the chairs that had been placed nearby in the sand while taking in the beauty that enveloped us in the silence all around. The sky was a brilliant tableau of colours and the stars overwhelmed us with the beauty of it all. I felt choked with emotion. It was the perfect time to meditate, so we began our ceremony by playing the music of Isis and sipped a small amount of red wine to symbolise our communion with Jesus Christ. Through our meditation, our awareness of Christ consciousness became more profound and we felt very connected to Mother Earth and to our higher selves. The Milky Way loomed overhead as we sent out Reiki universal life force energy to spread love, light and peace to the world; it was as if the sky was descending on us, urging us to create a connection with the universe. I felt I could reach out and touch the stars, as they were so low. It was a wonderful experience for us both, which kept us awake until 4 am.

General view of the night sky over a camp in Wadi Rum. Photo by Omar Sawalha

When we eventually woke up the next morning, I looked out of the window and gasped, for there, in plain sight, was a steep drop on the other side of the window. There is no way someone could have climbed up and knocked at the window. I pondered on that thought for a moment when Donna said she felt that the spirits had woken us up to meditate under a starlit sky to experience Christ consciousness. I stood and gazed out of the window in quiet contemplation as my eyes took in the beauty of Mother Nature in all her glory; the sacredness of this place transcended time. It was blissful, and I felt the vastness of peace within me because I was connected to the higher source. I stepped outside to stand in the sunlight and to breathe in the fresh air as if I was breathing in the light of the universe. I told myself that I am one with the light, and the light is one with me, and I am in the hands of God. Christ consciousness is a state of mind that is at peace and still. To achieve this, one must practise quieting the mind through meditation. This allows you to be in control of your thoughts. It awakens the true identity of your being, which aligns with a higher consciousness that opens the gateway to receiving thoughts from the higher source, the mind-set of Christ. With this newfound sense of bliss, we went to have breakfast, followed by a tour into the heart of the Wadi Rum desert that would bring our trip to a close.

The ride was a bit bumpy, but that was the least of our concerns, as a huge tornado of dust appeared to be heading straight towards us. The driver stopped the vehicle abruptly as we tried to find cover the best we could in an open truck, wrapping our scarves around our heads, but it was useless. The sandstorm appeared to target us as it swirled all around, buffeting the truck as we huddled in the corner, trying to breathe. It felt like a portal had opened for us to receive the energy from the wind. I viewed this as a blessing following our meditation ceremony the previous night and began to relax. This strange occurrence lasted for several minutes and then the wind disappeared as quickly as it came, and a complete calmness surrounded us. Despite being covered in a layer of pink dust, we cleaned up the best we could and continued on our journey.

The truck finally stopped at the edge of a cliff. We climbed out and sat down on a rock to take in the view. The Bedouin guide walked over to me, bent down and put his hand into the sand, then rubbed the damp, red sand onto my cheeks. I thought it was strange and wondered why he was doing that. He just smiled knowingly. There was no water anywhere to be seen, but the sand felt damp and moist. Then he did the same to Donna. We both knew it was a special healing as if we had been anointed.

We got back into the truck and were driven to a Bedouin tent, where we enjoyed a nice cup of sweet mint tea. One of the young Bedouin boys came up to us with a beaming smile and put frankincense oil on both our wrists. 'What's that all about?' I then remembered that frankincense is significant to Jesus, as it was one of the gifts from the Three Wise Men.

That unique time in the desert made me understand the reason why we had to visit Wadi Rum. It was because we had to receive the blessings of Christ consciousness to guide us towards the work we were destined to do. We felt we

Donna (left) and me anointed with sand on our cheeks in Wadi Rum

had received a divine blessing from the higher source as we carried out the ceremonies we were guided to perform. The red wine symbolised the blood of Jesus that was shed for humanity; the oil of frankincense was a spiritual anointment that signified the Holy Spirit; the meditation music signified that the goddess Isis was symbolically guiding and healing us throughout the ceremony. We also witnessed the four elements: *air* when the sand and wind swirled around us; *water and earth* when the Bedouin guide put the moist red sand on our cheeks; and the campfire used for our evening meal symbolised the *fire* element.

The next morning, we left the camp and headed further south for Aqaba on the Red Sea, the only seaport in Jordan. We arrived at the hotel and were received by a lovely Filipino lady dressed all in red, complete with red stiletto-heeled shoes; she was so welcoming. She checked us into our room, which had a beautiful balcony with stunning sea views. I registered her name on her badge and thanked her. Once again, we were given our sign: the colour red.

We headed to the beach to soak up the sun, and after a few hours, we decided to take a tour on a glass bottomed-boat to see the fish and corals. When the boatman came, he asked, "Only two of you?" I thanked the heavens that he did not refuse to take us, and he stopped the boat where we asked him to go. We had a spectacular view of the fish and corals. Donna jumped into the sea to cool off in the crystal clear waters; I just stayed on the boat. I don't particularly like swimming in the deep blue sea without a life jacket, and I was content to stay on the boat and breathe in the sweet sea air.

When we returned to shore, the heat was so unbearable that we headed for the restaurant to quench our thirst on a cooling glass of iced mint tea. We went to sit down at a table set up for the evening meal, but the waiter would not allow it. I was disappointed, so I went to the barman and asked if we could sit in the shade. He kindly obliged, moved the tablecloth off one of the tables, and served us with a big smile. We thanked him for his kindness and I took note of his name too, as I wanted to write a thank you letter to the manager praising his staff. We both slept very well that night.

In the morning, I gave my letter to the girl dressed in red at the reception desk as we went in for breakfast. When we were about to walk to the buffet, a waitress came to our table and served us the most delicious food that saved us time lining up at the buffet. I looked at the name on her badge; her name was Mary. We both looked at each other knowingly, as the name Mary was connected to our spiritual experience with Jesus in the Wadi Rum desert.

As we were leaving the hotel, we saw the manager meeting with the people I wrote about in my letter. They turned towards us and gave us a 'thumbs up;' their happy smiling faces said it all. Donna was right. We certainly received the red carpet treatment with red rose petals all the way. God works in mysterious ways, especially when you are doing sacred work.

I believe that all things happen for a reason. Nothing during our lifetime is meaningless or without purpose, even though that purpose is not always revealed to us. If you believe that the universe provides constant signs of divine grace and you pay attention to them, you have been guided by the universe to be in touch with your higher self. When this happens, one can see miracles all around.

Many people believe in miracles because they want to think they take place. It is up to each individual to decide whether a miracle has happened. The truth in this answer lies in the fact that people seek out hope, and we all need hope in these difficult times. By looking at miracles through divine understanding, you will be provided with the evidence of God's presence and power in the world. This is especially true in cases involving loved ones who suffer illness or injury. Regardless of the religion and creed you follow, if you remain open-minded to this divine source, you will also witness extraordinary happenings. This happened to me when I saw my brother recover from stage four cancer, as you will read in the next chapter.

Chapter 10

REGGIE – MY BROTHER

THE SPIRITUAL EXPERIENCE AND BLESSINGS I received in Wadi Rum in 2018 served me well over the following year. I felt more attuned to God's divine grace. Perhaps I was being prepared for my next journey to England, in June of 2019. I had just received a troubling email from my twin sister Tudy, who informed me that my brother Reggie was going to have surgery for stage four cancer of the lungs and lymph nodes. I was quite upset to read this, as my mother had died of lung cancer all those years ago. I went to meditate in my room and almost immediately, my higher self told me, 'Go to Reggie.' Later that day, I replied to Tudy and asked if I could stay with her for three weeks. "Of course!" she replied excitedly, as we had not seen each other for many years.

I booked my ticket and began to prepare for my trip. One of the first things I was guided to do was to visit the Church of Saint George in Salt (*see chapter 6*), and to take with me the rosary beads I had bought a few years ago from the church at the Baptism site. On arrival, I went straight to the special shrine, coated the beads with the holy oil that drips continuously from the wall of the cave, and then sat down and prayed for Reggie.

I set off for England, and as soon as I arrived at my sister's house in Billingham in the north of England, I told her that I wanted to give the rosary beads to Reggie. "Don't be silly, he doesn't believe in things like that!" she said. But I knew better and as my higher self told me to give them to him, I decided that I would do just that when the time was right. When we visited Reggie in the hospital the next day, I was saddened to see him in such pain despite the morphine he had been given following a long, tough surgery. "Reggie, Susie is here from Jordan," said Tudy. He turned his face towards mine and gave me a beautiful smile; he was so happy to see me after such a long time.

After one week, I told Tudy that I wanted to give Reggie the blessing of Reiki universal energy, even though he would not understand it, as he was too ill. Every day for the next four days, I sat at home and gave Reggie an attunement blessing of Reiki and passed it on to him through distant healing. I warned Tudy to be prepared in case Reggie had physical reactions from the attunements, such as sweating and diarrhoea. This was to be expected in Reggie's case because his body was getting rid of all the poisons and toxins associated with his chemotherapy treatments. I looked over at my sister sitting at the kitchen table; she looked tired and pale. "I see you are not using Reiki on yourself. You are a Reiki master teacher, so why are you not using it?" I asked. Tudy was as spiritual as I was, being my twin. And then she explained that she found it hard to make time for herself, as she was also visiting Reggie's wife, who was suffering from dementia and being cared for in a home.

It was difficult to see my family having to cope with both mental and physical pain, so I suggested to Tudy that we give ourselves daily hands-on healing while I was in the UK, and she agreed. Every day after that, we took 20 minutes for ourselves to clear all the chakras and give ourselves an energy booster for the day. When Reggie came out of the hospital, I knew it would take a long time for him to recuperate, as he looked so weak and could barely walk. "God bless him," I said as we helped him into a chair. "Look, Reggie, I got these rosary beads from the Saint John the Baptist Church at the site where Jesus was baptised. Would you like them?" I asked him. "They have been blessed with holy oil from a church in Jordan where some people have experienced miracles." His eyes lit up as I offered him the rosary beads. He took them eagerly and instantly put them around his neck. "Susie, do you know I pray to Virgin Mary every day," he replied with pride. Tudy stood in stunned silence and said in a quiet voice, "Really, Reggie? I never knew."

I had been back in Jordan for a few months when I received the happy news from Tudy that Reggie was completely cured. Even the doctors thought it was a miracle. I knew that his power of faith and belief, along with my gift of the blessed rosary beads, had contributed to Reggie's recovery. It really was a miracle and all was well on the home front until one year later when I received a message from Tudy informing me that our older sister, Ann – who lived in Spain – had sustained life-threatening injuries in a bad fall. I rang Ann every other day and even though she could hardly breathe or speak, I knew it gave her comfort, as we were unable to reach her only son to inform him of his mother's condition. The doctor warned us it was a matter of time, but she hung on until she heard her son's voice. We eventually found him and he called his mother for the last time on 1st August 2020. Later that day, I prayed to my own mother, 'please take Ann and let her pass with no pain.' That night, Ann passed away in her sleep – finally at peace. She did not make it to her 76th birthday on 6th August, but I knew she would celebrate it with my mother in the spirit world.

Chapter 11

SAINT CHARBEL

A Patron Saint of Lebanon

ON 20TH JUNE 2020, A CLIENT arrived for her Grand Master Reiki course. While in my healing room during the initiation, she suddenly asked, "Who is that man in the picture on your wall?" "That's Saint Charbel. I got it as a gift in 2018," I told her. "He was a Lebanese Maronite Christian monk who lived during the nineteenth century."

Saint Charbel Makhlouf (1828-1898) obtained a wide reputation for holiness as he dedicated himself to a monastic life that combined prayer, silence and asceticism. In 1977, he was canonised by Pope Paul VI, who described him as an "admirable flower of sanctity blooming on the stem of the ancient monastic traditions of the East."[21] His sanctuary is located at the Monastery of Saint Maron-Annaya in the north of Lebanon.[22] Saint Charbel is considered the patron saint of Lebanon and known as the 'miracle monk' and protector by his followers for the many miraculous healings they have received in answer to their prayers.

"Well, he's here now," my client said, "and he's all dressed in blue and telling me to tell you he wants you to go to him; he wants to talk to you." How could I go to his shrine in Lebanon? Especially now with all the political upheaval happening there, not to mention Covid restrictions … and I carried on with the initiation, trying to put that thought behind me.

---

[21] https://www.catholicnewsagency.com/saint/st-charbel-makhlouf-534
[22] http://www.saintcharbel.com/home.php?lgid=0

That thought stayed with me a few days longer. I could not stop thinking about the chat I had with my client, and then it occurred to me. I remembered there was a Maronite church in Amman dedicated to Saint Charbel. So with my group of spiritual friends we set off to visit the church. When we arrived, I was drawn to a lovely painting of Saint Charbel that covered the wall behind the altar. I said out loud, "Well, I'm here," as I did not know what to expect.

I was then guided to sit in front of the altar in the middle of the church. While doing so, I glanced upwards and saw a beautiful painting of Saint Charbel on the high up on the wall and he was wearing his characteristic black robe. I sat for a while in quiet contemplation, and as I looked back at his painting on the ceiling, I could see clearly that Saint Charbel's robe was no longer black but blue. I thought back to the words my client had told me the week before; was this the sign I needed?

I paused in my seat trying to understand what I had just witnessed, when my higher self told me to walk over to the altar. I wondered why, as nothing was there except for a white tablecloth. When I reached the altar, I then understood, as there was a small cross, embroidered in red on the lower corner of the tablecloth. 'What's he trying to tell me?' I wondered.

I then recalled the vision I had back in 2010, when I saw myself standing next to Mary during the crucifixion of Jesus. That was the day I saw the red cross on my kitchen counter while making my husband's breakfast. It looked exactly the same, which made me realise the signs I keep receiving were to reassure me that I am following my destiny ordained by God.

On our way home, we took a detour to the lovely grotto of the Virgin Mary at the St Mary of Nazareth Church in west Amman. I had never been but had been told how beautiful it was and I really wanted to see it. When we arrived, the grotto was lit up in blue and the energy emanating from this small space was very special. After visiting the grotto, my higher self told me to walk around to the back of the church, but my friends said there was nothing there.

"Well, I'm going to look anyway," I said and as I turned the corner of the church, there before me was a statue of Saint Charbel within a small cave. We stood in amazed silence, as we had no idea this shrine existed.

Painting on the wall behind the altar of the Maronite Church of Saint Charbel, Amman

I searched for the reason why I have this connection with Saint Charbel. Ever since I was gifted a picture of him, I can feel his presence in my house. Has he come to guide me and to work through me in my Reiki healings? Perhaps this is because he was the miracle monk who was renowned for his healings. And so from that day on, I have accepted his spiritual guidance in my life and I pray to Saint Charbel to use me as a tool and to work through me when I do my Reiki healings.

I am sure that if each one of you listens to your higher self – that little voice within – you will also experience the things I have written about in this book. Don't doubt the signs that God gives you; believe in them, as they are divine messages for your well-being to guide you on your path in life. We call it

Me at Saint Charbel's grotto, St Mary of Nazareth Church, Amman

'synchronicity' and it took a moment of self-doubt to understand its true meaning. One morning, feeling overwhelmed, I asked my mother in the spirit world why she made me write this book. Five minutes later, I found out why, as

I received a message on my phone from a friend who sent me a spirit message card for daily guidance titled: 'synchronicity,' and it read:

"Are you noticing the signs of synchronicity that the Spirit World has been sending to you at this time? People and situations in your life are not just appearing by coincidence; in reality, they're being guided to you from the Spirit World to help you for a specific reason. Synchronicities are blessings and signs of grace that are not just mere coincidences, but are evidence that you are and always will be connected to Spirit. When synchronicity appears in your life, it is usually a sign that you should look beyond the normal limitations of the physical and consider the spiritual meaning of what is or what is about to happen in your life. Synchronicity often puts certain people in your path, or gives you a particular book. The more you notice and pay attention to these meaningful signs of grace, the easier it is for them to multiply and give you spiritual guidance." [23]

It was reassuring to receive that card at that moment, as my mother was sending me a sign that my book was meant to be. Synchronicity happens for a reason, and it also helped me to look deeper into the direction of my life and to acknowledge the spiritual shift that was taking place. For me personally, synchronicity presents itself when people come in and out of my life to relay a message from the spirit world or to tell me where I am to go and what I am to do. Nothing in life is a coincidence, which I would discover when I met Nisreen one year later.

---

[23] The Spirit Messages Daily Guidance Oracle Deck by John Holland

Chapter 12

SYNCHRONICITY

IT WAS JUNE 2021, AND the pandemic was still with us, but we were learning to live with Covid-19, so my friends and I decided to visit the Baptism site. I felt drawn to go once again, however, I was not sure why. So, I went into my healing room to say a prayer to Mary, hoping to find the answer and asked her to show me something biblical while I was there, if it was my divine right.

The day before we left, I received a message from Donna in the UK telling me about an amazing group meditation session she had joined that morning. She explained that the group facilitator, Anya, asked everyone to meditate on a place they considered sacred. Donna had chosen the Baptism site in Jordan, while others Glastonbury and the Pyramids of Egypt. I told Donna we were visiting the Baptism site the next day, and she replied, "This is no coincidence, Susie, as I feel there is something you have to do there." Little did I know that the text I received from Donna the following day was possibly the reason why I had to go. Donna was guided to give me a prayer she had channelled that morning. She also told me that I would know where to offer the prayer.

When we arrived at the Baptism site and met up with our tour guide, we were fortunate, as there were no other tourists there that day. It was empty and peaceful as we walked along the trail towards the actual site where John baptised Jesus. The guide surprised us when he opened a small barrier and allowed us to descend the few steps down to this sacred place, where luckily, there was a small pool of water. It was the sign I needed, and it was here that I recited Donna's prayer:

"As you touch the water visualise all waterways on Mother Earth being gifted with God's loving healing energy. All sacred sites are being cleansed of any negative vibration and recharged with love and light, Christ's consciousness, and for peace to prevail for all sentient beings. Amen."

We felt so enlightened and blessed to have stood at this sacred place once again. We then continued our journey towards the River Jordan but were surprised at the sight of mud everywhere, which stopped us from reaching the riverbank. It had flooded the previous week and when the water level had receded, it left a mass of mud that blocked the passageway down to the River Jordan. Mother Nature had stopped us, which served to reconfirm that the prayer was offered at the right place. While walking back, a donkey suddenly appeared out of nowhere and followed us along the path. His face was so beautiful and it felt like he wanted to make his presence known to me. I then remembered my previous visit in 2010 when I felt I was walking in the footsteps of Jesus; a path Joseph, with Mary on a donkey, would have walked too. My prayer earlier that morning had been answered; Mary had honoured my wish and shown me a 'biblical' sign.

On the first anniversary of my sister Ann's death, 1st August 2021, it was a beautiful, sunny day as Donna and I along with our friend Louise, returned from a visit up north. As we passed Tel al-Ruman, I mentioned that I would like to go to church and light a candle for Ann when Louise suddenly said, "Oh look, Susie, there's a church over there." We parked the car inside the grounds of what turned out to be a Missionaries of Charity compound for the nuns of Mother Teresa. Although the church was closed, we walked around the beautiful garden where many statues of saints were displayed amongst the trees. We felt we were on a short pilgrimage to a very special place and were drawn to a small glass case containing a statue of the Virgin Mary. I walked over and opened the door and saw a red rose had been placed in her hand. This was a beautiful sign from my mother, letting me know that Ann was with her, for my mother's favourite flower was the red rose; it brought tears to my eyes. While walking around, we also noticed a beautiful statue of Mother Teresa holding a baby in her arms, as well as plaques placed around the garden with special spiritual verses on them, one of which read: *"The fruit of silence is prayer. The fruit of prayer is faith. The fruit of faith is love. The fruit of love is service. The fruit of service is peace."* While another read: *"We need to be alone with God in silence to be renewed and to be transformed."*

The red rose sign from my mother

As we continued to walk around the garden, a nun came out of her quarters waving at us with a big warm smile, and without a word, she went back inside. Shortly afterwards, we heard angelic singing that echoed all around us.

We then knew we were guided to find this holy site, as we all felt surrounded by divine, healing love and energy simply because music and song hold the sacred, vibrational power to heal, and they are an important part of a pilgrimage. We could not believe that this beautiful, peaceful sanctuary was here in Jordan and in what seemed to be the middle of nowhere.

The caretaker of the church then approached us and asked if we would like to go inside the church. "We would love to, thank you!" we all said. So I got my wish as I lit a candle and said a short prayer for my sister, Ann. We sat in front of the altar in peaceful meditation when Donna began spontaneously to sing 'Amazing Grace,' and we all joined in. The vibrational sound of our singing that echoed around the church filled me with bliss, a sense of healing that cured my sorrow; even the caretaker could feel the positive vibration all around us. When we had finished, the caretaker showed us around the church and pointed to a beautiful stained-glass window depicting two keys, one blue and one pink. I had never noticed keys on a church window before and took it as another sign that Ann had passed peacefully into heaven; it was very comforting. I later learnt that the two crossed keys symbolised the keys of the kingdom of heaven that Jesus gave to his disciple Peter to spread his divine teachings.[24] Although I feel connected spiritually to Jesus and the Virgin Mary, I believe we are all connected as one on Earth and we are all God's children regardless of the faith we embrace.

A few days later, a new client came to me for a Reiki course. Before we began, she noticed the Virgin Mary chain I was wearing around my neck, "You are very close to Mary," she said. "Yes," I replied, "You are right."

---

[24] https://en.wikipedia.org/wiki/Keys_of_Heaven

On the second day of the course, she surprised me even more when she said, "Did you know you were with Virgin Mary at the crucifixion of Jesus?" I then knew this person in front of me was special and very intuitive. I had not told anyone about the vision I had experienced back in 2010 when I saw myself standing at the crucifixion of Jesus. And yet, eleven years later, I find myself sitting opposite a complete stranger who tells me the same thing as if it were quite normal. She then asked me if I had pain in my left ankle. Once again, I was surprised and said, "Yes, I do, how do you know this?" She said that her higher self was telling her that I must go to Moses' springs at Mount Nebo, near the town of Madaba. She said the spring is one of the two places where Moses is believed to have obtained water by striking a rock. Six giant eucalyptus trees mark the spot, and an occasional waterfall trickles over the rocks. She told me that I needed to put my ankle in the spring water to be healed. As I have never been there, she offered to take me. And so began a friendship with Nisreen, a Muslim medical doctor who joined my spiritual circle of friends, and who, in the process, also became the channel through which I received messages from the blessed Virgin Mary.

A week later, it was the portal of the Lions' Gate on 8th August when the star Sirius perfectly aligned with Orion's Belt and the Pyramids of Egypt. Since the time of the ancient Egyptians, this cosmic shift has been celebrated worldwide for thousands of years as it brings transformation, spiritual awakening and prosperity. I felt it was the perfect day to go to Mount Nebo. When we arrived at Moses' springs, the ground was rather rough and hilly, and I was glad I had brought my special steel walking stick that I had used in Austria when I walked along the ancient pilgrimage path of Falkenstein.

Luckily, there appeared to be no one around Moses' spring that day as Nisreen led us down the rocky slope. We entered the cave where the fresh healing water trickled out of the rocks and collected in a small pool. I put my feet and the walking stick into this blessed, healing water; it felt so relaxing and refreshing. The others joined me as we all sat in a circle and spontaneously held each other's hands and began to meditate, sending Reiki universal energy to the world. The sounds of nature all around us, from the water trickling over the rocks to the birds chirping as they flew from water to tree, was a magical moment of bonding with Mother Nature. I felt so much gratitude and appreciation for everything that came my way.

Healing my ankle in the spring waters of Moses, Mount Nebo

Before we knew it, one hour had passed. I got up, picked up my walking stick and realised that I was walking better and my ankle was free of pain. I was about to tell Louise when she suddenly turned and went up the hill to help a woman wearing a traditional long dress struggling to descend. She had a small 5-year-old child with her, who was very boisterous. When they arrived at the springs, we noticed that her son had Down's syndrome and kept his distance. However, as soon as he saw my walking stick he grabbed it from me, holding onto it with both hands. He was completely still and quiet, which surprised his mother more than me. We asked her if we could give him healing. She nodded 'yes' as we gathered around him and placed our hands on his head as we gave him Reiki, universal life force energy. After five minutes, he let go of the stick and stood quietly beside his mother. We felt he could sense the power and the positive energy that emanated from my walking stick; it was a blessing to witness. His mother was so happy and grateful that her son had reacted so positively to the healing that she invited us all for lunch. She explained to Nisreen the medical problems she had with her son, who refused to let anyone near him or touch him. We were the first people to do so outside of his immediate family. We felt humbled by this and did not want to burden the boy's mother, so we politely declined her offer, said our goodbyes and made our way to the top of the hill. We sat down to watch the magnificent sunset and absorb the events of the day. Again, I felt so blessed to be at this miraculous place on this special day; we had indeed witnessed a significant shift in consciousness and healing.

No sooner had we returned from our memorable trip to Moses' spring waters than we were preparing another trip, this time to a special place in religious history – the Cave of the Seven Sleepers. The parable surrounding this particular cave has endured the test of time according to Byzantine and Islamic ancient sources[25]. It recalls the story of several pious young men – and a dog – who sought refuge in a cave to escape Christian persecution under Roman Emperor Decius around 250 AD. According to the story, they woke up a few hundred years later, only to find that the world had changed and Christianity had become the official religion of the Roman Empire, following the Edict of Milan in 313 AD. Although the actual location of this cave is controversial, the

---

[25] https://wikiislam.net/wiki/Seven_Sleepers_of_Ephesus_in_the_Quran; a 5th century Christian legend used to emphasise the ability of the Christian faith to overcome persecution and to celebrate the Christianisation of the Roman Empire. The story of the companions of the cave is also found in the 18th surah of the Qur'an, *Al-Kahf* (The Cave).

two main archaeological sites connected to this parable can be found in Turkey and Jordan. Today, they have both become major pilgrimage sites.

Keen to experience the positive energy that can be felt at the Jordanian site, we set off on August 18th and discovered it was only a short car ride to the Cave of the Seven Sleepers (*Ashab al Kahf ar–Raqim*) in East Amman. When we arrived, we changed into the Islamic prayer robes and scarves required to enter the cave and waited in line. After listening to a brief description of the site's history, we went inside with a large group of visitors. But we did not stay for long and left, with nothing special to report and no sign of Nisreen, who had disappeared briefly. When she returned, she told us she had asked the Imam (one who leads Muslim worshippers in prayer) for permission to go back into the cave by ourselves and he had agreed. Once the last visitor had left, we re-entered the cave and began to meditate. Meanwhile, the Imam started spontaneously reciting the Qur'an; it felt and sounded like God's divine energy was vibrating throughout this space and embracing us. The vibrations from the Qur'anic recital penetrated every pore of our bodies as tears rolled uncontrollably down our faces. At that moment, it was as if time stood still, for we were all one, under the grace of God. This place and its story became yet another link to Christ consciousness and pure peace for the mind, the body and the soul.

Even though we did not understand the words the Imam was saying, the pure vibrational sound that enveloped us as the Imam recited the Qur'an gave more meaning to this visit. I felt my mind, body and soul were being healed. It was a blessing that was one of the most serene moments I have ever known, and it served to reinforce my belief that there is a power greater than us on Earth.

If you remain open to the signs the universe is sending you, it will align you with the people who match your own vibrational energy. The more you develop your self-belief and raise your vibration, the more you will experience situations and friendships that benefit your well-being.

Chapter 13

THE WINTER SOLSTICE

WINTER WAS APPROACHING; THE COOL breeze everywhere was a refreshing sign that summer had passed, at least for another few months. I was looking forward to trips up to the hilly north of Jordan, an area of outstanding natural beauty known in ancient times as 'Gilead.' This region has a long history of the rise and fall of empires that left behind the ruins of many forts, castles and early churches. In particular, part of this area was known as the 'Decapolis' – a group of ten ancient Greco-Roman cities that were formed after the Roman conquest of Palestine in 63 BC. Five of these cities are located here, which include: Jerash (Gerasa), Umm Qais (Gadara), Tabaqat Fahl (Pella), and Qweilbeh (Raphana or Abila), further south is the sixth, modern-day Amman, the capital city of Jordan then known as Philadelphia. Some of the Decapolis cities are also mentioned in the New Testament Bible in the gospels of Matthew, Mark and Luke as locations where Jesus travelled, "healing all kinds of sickness" (Matthew 4:23-25).

Although Ajloun was not one of the Decapolis cities, it must have benefitted from the ancient trade routes that crisscrossed the region. Today, the town benefits from many archaeological sites that welcome pilgrims from all over the world. I often visit Ajloun and we were all looking forward to another visit on 21st December 2021, the day of the winter solstice. However, a turn of events was about to give deeper meaning to this visit.

Early in December, Nisreen rang to tell me about a vision she had during a meditation session. A monk appeared to her and told me we were all to go to the 'church' at Tel Mar Elias, where we would find 'the three different religions as one.' He further told her that we would see a miracle while we were there, as well as the colour 'red.'

Tel Mar Elias is the site of two large Byzantine churches that were built in the sixth century AD. It is located on a hill overlooking Ajloun near the village of Al Wahadneh. This village, also known as Khirbet Mar Elias, is believed to be the residence and possibly even the birthplace of Elijah, a prophet revered by Muslims, Christians and Jews.

I had not expected to receive such a divine message, as we had visited this site the month before. While I was there, I had left my red apple in a nook of a wall by the ruins of the church, where there were many birds and squirrels. I thought I would leave it for them to eat. I wondered why we had to return to Tel Mar Elias, then put that thought to the back of my mind and went to have lunch with Donna. It was a very cold, wet and windy day, but I did not mind, as Jordan needed the rain badly.

While at lunch, my higher self told me that we had to return to St Mary of Nazareth Church in west Amman, so we hurried to pay the bill and headed straight to Mary's grotto in the grounds of the church. I experienced what I can only describe as a tangible blessing from Mary. Her spirit seemed to embrace us as we prayed, as I felt a tingling sensation go through every pore within my body. It was as if she was standing right next to me. I have always been conscious of Mary's presence – protecting, guiding and loving me throughout my life.

Before leaving the church, I took a photo of Mary's statue. Unbeknownst to us, there was a strange light in one of the photographs that I shared with a friend. "What's that white light that looks like a stick in Mary's hand?" she asked me. Donna and I had not noticed it before until she pointed it out. I then realised this was the symbolic sign that meant I had to return with my walking stick to receive the energy from Mary. I also realised this had to be done before our trip to Ajloun for the winter solstice.

The morning of 21st December arrived and before departing for Ajloun, we all went to Mary's grotto in the St Mary of Nazareth Church. I brought my walking stick and placed it next to Mary's hand to receive her divine energy. While in the grotto, my higher self told me to take three candles with me to Ajloun. So I left a donation in the church box, and armed with the three candles, we continued on our journey to complete the winter solstice ceremony. On this day, many people worldwide perform similar ceremonies to spread light and healing to humanity and Mother Earth.

My walking stick receiving divine energy at St Mary of Nazareth Church grotto

We arrived at Tel Mar Elias on a gloomy day. As we stood admiring the view over the mountains, a large flock of white doves appeared overhead and formed a circle. They flew around us three times and then disappeared into the horizon; it was magical. We walked over to a large ancient wishing tree near the apse of the church ruins, where pilgrims still leave prayer ribbons. The colourful pieces of cloth tied to the branches of the tree show that, to this day, Tel Mar Elias is revered as a very holy place.

We stood in the open under a sky heavy with grey clouds when a beam of blue light suddenly began to shine down on us from a gap in the clouds. We took this as the sign to begin our ceremony as if the pillars of light opened up a portal to activate the divine energy for Mother Earth. We all stood in a circle and held my walking stick while praying and sending Reiki energy into the Earth. When we had finished, we opened our eyes and found that a mystical white fog had surrounded us; there was no separation between the Earth and the sky, just stillness of pure white energy that felt like we had been transported into another magical dimension. We took a moment to give thanks for this humbling experience and then walked down to the other archaeological church site. There, I noticed a picture of Jesus that someone had placed carefully in what looked like a little altar within the rocks. I knew then where to light my three candles for 'the three different religions as one.'

When we finally finished and were ready to go home, something red caught my eye on the wall. It was the red apple that I had put there a month ago! I suddenly felt that the apple symbolised where it had all begun, before the story of Adam and Eve and before the scriptures had been passed on to people. It was a time when people were all one. As the story of Adam and Eve is part of the teachings of all three Abrahamic religions – Judaism, Christianity and Islam – I saw the apple symbolically connecting all three faiths that were represented by the three candles I had just lit. The miracle was that despite the apple being there for a while, it was still wholesome and untouched by time.

'How amazing,' I thought, when we suddenly heard a very loud boom of thunder overhead; it was as if God was thanking us for what we had accomplished that day.

The sky over Tel Mar Elias with the blue sign

A few days later, we were guided to visit a sacred site in the north of the country. We did not know where this was, so we got out the map and realised it was the sacred site of Al-Buqayawiyya, more specifically a 'blessed tree.' It was located near the Jordanian-Iraqi border, over 150 km from Amman. On 28th December, we set off to visit the Tree of Al Buqayawiyya, which stands alone in a vast empty desert landscape, marking the once thriving ancient trade and caravan routes between the Hijaz and Syria.

This magnificent pistachio tree is referred to as the 'living *Sahabi*' – a living companion of the Prophet Muhammad (peace be upon him) – which tells us the story of a Syrian Nestorian Christian monk, known as Bahira[26], who prophesied the coming of the Prophet Muhammad (pbuh). It is believed that

---

[26] https://en.wikipedia.org/wiki/Bahira

the young Muhammad had accompanied his uncle, Abu Taleb, on a trade caravan route to Syria and that they had taken a rest under the shade of this tree. Bahira, who lived nearby, noticed the child and told Abu Taleb to take care of the boy and protect him from any enemies he might find along the route, for he was the Prophet 'that will come at the end of time.'

Tel Mar Elias and my red apple

We finally arrived at our destination and were greeted by a barren landscape with no vegetation, no water, no nothing, except for this ancient tree that stood before us devoid of leaves; naturally, of course, because it was winter. By springtime, it would be covered in lush green leaves. We were amazed at how this tree had survived in such a harsh environment for so long. Of course, we should have known better, as we reminded ourselves that it was a unique and blessed tree that had sheltered the Prophet Muhammad (pbuh) as a young boy.

Once again, we were guided to do a sacred ceremony at this special site and as we began, a flock of birds suddenly appeared out of nowhere and landed on the tree, creating a whirlwind all around us. They stayed for a good five minutes and then they were gone. We stood in silence and felt that we were standing in front of something divine. Despite its lack of leaves, the energy emanating from the tree left us feeling at peace, in harmony with our surroundings, and full of bliss, love and joy. It was as if we were in paradise, even though the area was desolate.

Aware that this sacred tree should not be touched, we gathered a few twigs that had fallen to the ground, which Nisreen planted in her garden the next day around the base of an old, tired tree. A week later, Nisreen phoned to tell me that, to her surprise and great joy, new shoots had sprouted in her garden where she had planted the twigs from the blessed tree. But more than that, she also noticed that on the bark of her tired old tree, a faint image of Mary had appeared, as if to welcome her. I just had to go and see for myself, so Donna and I left for Nisreen's garden. She was right. As we stood before the tree, we could clearly see the image of Mary on the bark of the trunk.

We gathered around and began to meditate. Collectively, we felt pure joy and experienced the oneness of all, to the point where it brought tears to our eyes. I began to wonder, out loud, why we had to go to all the places we were guided to visit. Was it the outpouring of emotion that led me to another fleeting moment of self-doubt?

I got my answer a week later when Mary appeared to Nisreen during a meditation. Nisreen asked her the same question and she replied that it was our mission in this life to spread God's love and light to Mother Earth. This was the confirmation I needed to explain why I felt so connected to the spirit of Jesus and the blessed Virgin Mary.

The Blessed Tree of Al-Buqayawiyya, in the winter

Close-up of the tree trunk with an image of Mary

Chapter 14

PETRA, JABAL HAROUN

FOR THE PREVIOUS YEAR, DONNA and I had planned to go on a pilgrimage to visit Aaron's tomb deep within the Sharah mountain range of Petra, but we were stopped for one reason or another.

Ten months later, a few days after I received a message of spiritual guidance from Saint Charbel, I found myself climbing the steep slopes of Jabal Haroun, along with Donna, Nisreen and Louise, on 29th October 2022.

According to ancient religious sources and traditions, Jabal Haroun (Arabic for Aaron's Mountain) is said to be the biblical Mount Hor, where Aaron, the brother of Moses, died and was buried. Since the time of the Nabateans, over two thousand years ago, until the present, it has remained a site of inter-religious pilgrimage for people of the region and beyond.

In September 2022, I received a client for a Reiki session and we began to talk about Saint Charbel's shrine in Lebanon that she planned to visit later that month. I told her I had always wanted to go there, so I was pleasantly surprised when she rang me a few weeks afterwards and told me she had a gift for me. She arrived at my house carrying with her a bottle of holy oil and incense from the shrine of Saint Charbel in Lebanon, as well as a replica of the white belt that he wore around his robe and a small sample of soil from his grave. I was very touched by her kind gesture and the fact that she remembered our conversation. A few weeks later, while healing myself in my healing room, Saint Charbel came through to me and told me that seven of us would go to Aaron's tomb on 29th October and that I was to take with me the gifts I had received from his shrine. It was divine timing that led us to plan our trip for that weekend.

On the morning of 28th October, I woke up with anticipation and looked at the clock; it was 6:11 am. I looked up the meaning of 611, which gave me chapter six, verse eleven of the Gospel of Matthew in the New Testament. I felt it was interesting as it refers to the Sermon on the Mount, and we were heading south to a mountain that morning. As the number 611 is an angel number, its appearance was a message of encouragement, a sign of synchronicity that meant my prayers had been answered and that I was being guided along the right path. When I met up with Nisreen and Donna, they told me that they had both woken up at 5:11 am – the symbolism of this would show itself to us later that day.

We began our journey by car to Aaron's tomb, which stands on top of Jabal Haroun, the highest peak in the Petra region at 1,350 metres above sea level. Along the way, Donna mentioned that she had received a meditation from Anya, an angelic and galactic channeller and healer from the UK, who confirmed to her why she had to be with me on this sacred journey. While in the car, we listened to Anya's meditation, which lasted for forty-three minutes. Anya felt strongly connected to the sacred journey we were about to go on, as she was channelling and anchoring a beautiful golden light. She said, 'give and you shall receive.'

The meditation helped to ground us through visualising a lapis lazuli crystal in the centre of the Earth. Anya then explained the importance of spiritual healing by avoiding low negative vibrations. As Anya continued to speak, she talked about a vision she had of blue and yellow windows and a golden ring of protection around Mother Earth. She went on to say how all these new portals will be opened and activated on Earth to spread peace and light to humanity. At the very end of her channelling, she asked us to go out into nature and, if possible, to hug a tree, at which point Ahmed, our driver, pulled over to the side of the road for a break and to have breakfast. We hadn't realised the car had stopped; we felt at peace from the meditation we had just finished. When we finally became aware of our surroundings, we noticed that Ahmad had stopped the car next to a group of trees. We got out of the car and hugged a tree absorbing Mother Nature's energy. It was a peaceful experience.

We continued on our journey, driving south along the King's Highway and almost at our destination, we passed by Shobak Castle, the first of the crusader castles built in Jordan in 1115 AD. Nisreen asked if we would like to visit it, and we all said, "Yes!" As we turned off the highway, we passed a small VW beetle car on the side of the road, famously known as 'the smallest hotel in the world'. We all thought it was amusing and stopped to say hello to the owner. Next to the car, there was a table full of crystals that the owner's son was selling. We were all drawn to a few aqua blue andara glass crystals that have been used for centuries to heal negative energy. I realised they were the same as the crystal I always carry in my handbag, and we were guided to buy one each. While drinking a cup of tea, the young boy came over with a big smile on his face and gifted us each a beautiful necklace of coloured gems, like the colour of a rainbow. Despite our attempts to pay him, he refused to accept any money, so we decided to stay for lunch. Anya was right again, 'give and you shall receive.'

Just when we were about to leave, an old Bedouin man came up and tapped on the window of our car. "Hello," he said, smiling. We returned his kind greeting and noticed the number '511' printed in English on the front of his jacket. We thought no more of it as we continued on for the short drive to Wadi Musa (Valley of Moses in Arabic), a town above a valley that surrounds Petra. Right at the entrance to the town is Moses' spring, where, according to history, Moses struck the rock and brought forth water. We felt compelled to visit. We entered the small structure built around the spring, where we found, as Anya had said, bright blue windows with golden sunlight all around us. I placed the aquamarine crystals onto the rock, where I also put my walking stick to receive this blessed energy, and then we sat and meditated with our feet in the small stream that trickled into a small pool. There was nobody there except a young boy who was fascinated by what we were doing. He kept trying to touch my walking stick and the crystals, so I let him because, to me, he physically felt the energy that was emanating from my walking stick; the innocence of a child is shown in many ways. While we collected a small bottle of this spring water to take with us on our journey, Donna looked up and noticed some graffiti on the wall in red paint. It was the number 511, again in English, and this time we took note. This sign was an affirmation that we were on the right path; '511' is also an angel number symbolising intense spiritual growth and enlightenment.

'The smallest hotel in the world', with Shobak Castle in the background

When we arrived at our hotel in Wadi Musa, we walked through a beautiful garden full of flowers with birds singing in the trees; it was like a garden of paradise in the middle of the desert and it was heartwarming. While waiting for our keys at the reception, I noticed a beautifully carved wooden statue of the Virgin Mary right opposite me. It was a reassuring sign of synchronicity that I would make it to Aaron's tomb, as She would be with me on my spiritual journey.

That night, as we sat outside on an open terrace to discuss the programme for the next day's big climb up Aaron's Mountain, we all heard the *mu'ethin* call the Muslim faithful to prayer. A most beautiful and mystical sound filled the air all around. While looking up at the sky, we saw the letter 'M' (as in the name of the Prophet Mohammad, pbuh) and the word 'Allah' in Arabic form in the clouds. We were amazed and saw this as a sign that our trip was blessed.

We left at 6:30 am the following day to begin our trek into Petra's magnificent valley (*siq*). After arriving at the Treasury, we hired a horse and carriage to take us to the meeting point 5 km away for our climb up the mountain, however, had we known it would be such a horrendously uncomfortable trip that gave us all a lot of aches and pains in our hips and backs, we would have walked, despite the distance, to meet our Bedouin guide. We finally met our wonderful and friendly Bedouin lady guide and her young niece, who would accompany us, along with Ahmad, our driver, up the mountain. Just as in my vision, seven of us climbed the mountain that day and we were blessed to have the energy of the wise Bedouin lady and the young, innocent energy of her niece. As we walked towards Aaron's Mountain, the sight before us filled us with panic, as we did not know if we could climb this enormous rock face. We could see Aaron's tomb miles away in the distance. It looked like it was in the heavens. Just as we decided we would take one step at a time and go as far as we could, a beautiful golden-yellow butterfly appeared, fluttering around us, lightening our mood. It also jogged my memory, as we had been told that the area around Jabal Haroun was closely associated with the goddess Isis. I then realised why I had been guided to bring with me the ascended master's card of Isis; she would be with us, her Mother Earth energy protecting us on our journey. Thus began our ascent of this mystical mountain steeped in religious history. It was a challenging climb, hampered by aches and pains, and we began to wonder if we would make it to the top of the highest mountain in Petra. I needn't have worried though, as our ailments began to disappear one by one as the day progressed. It was then that I realised all the prayers and energy my walking stick had absorbed over the last year helped me face the enormous challenge of climbing the mountain at the young age of 73! I felt blessed beyond words as if I was carried up that mountain on the wings of an angel.

Me in the white t-shirt walking up Jabal Haroun

We eventually reached a plateau 70 metres below the summit where Aaron's tomb lay. On this level are the remains of a fifth-century monastery, church and chapel dedicated to Aaron. I later learnt that archaeologists had discovered the ruins of a first-century Nabatean temple under the church, which meant that this mountain had been revered since the time of the Nabatean pagans too.[27] We paused to take in the sight of these ancient ruins before continuing our journey to the summit, following in the footsteps of many pilgrims who had been climbing this mountain for millennia.

Almost there! Approaching Aaron's tomb on Jabal Haroun

[27]https://www.researchgate.net/publication/287866744_From_Goddess_to_Prophet_2000_Years_of_Continuity_on_the_Mountain_of_Aaron_near_Petra_Jordan#pf19

We had finally arrived at Aaron's tomb and we were in awe of our achievements and the amazing view that greeted us for miles around. It was one of the most mystical journeys I have ever experienced in my whole life. We all felt we were connecting with one of the most spiritual places on Earth. The high vibrational energy that I felt was uplifting and unique and I stood in contemplative silence, absorbing it all; I felt healed. It was easy to see why pilgrims of all three monotheistic religions revere this sacred space. Slowly, we entered the tomb and were guided to join hands, connecting our energy to each other as we prayed, sending a circle of light around Mother Earth. This spiritually powerful experience gave me a heightened sense of consciousness and connection to the higher source, enhancing the light I sent to humanity.

View from the summit of Jabal Haroun, overlooking the monastic complex

As we emerged from the tomb into the bright sunlight, we noticed three signs of affirmation and synchronicity: The first one was seeing a ginger-coloured dog sitting on the rocks that came over to greet us, wagging his tail with happiness. We had just heard from Donna's meditation teacher, Anya, that her beloved pet dog, a golden retriever, had recently died. We knew that Anya felt a strong connection to our journey and the dog seemed to reinforce that spiritual connection with her.

The dog we met near the summit of Jabal Haroun

The second sign was a large beetle that appeared on the wall of the external staircase of the tomb that Donna was trying to climb. I might not have seen it if Donna had managed to climb to the top; however, she stopped halfway up, afraid to continue. When I looked up to check on her, out of the corner of my eye, I saw the beetle on the wall. It reminded me of the beetle I had come across in China; perhaps it was another message of thanks from the underworld.

The final sign came when Donna mentioned that while in the tomb, she repeatedly received a spiritual message that told her, "We have the keys" and "we are the keys." We thought this meant we needed a sign that we were on the right path. After regaining our energy, we returned to the lower level through the rock-cut staircase. We felt the serene tranquillity of the energy of this sacred spot and looked for a place to stamp the energy of my walking stick into the ground to spread God's love and light to Mother Earth.

It was our lovely golden-yellow butterfly, which never left our side that guided us towards the church. It was there, on one of the rocks, where Donna found an old rusty key pointing towards the butterfly; it was as though the key was waiting for Donna and it was our third sign of affirmation that we had arrived at our destination. Yet, it was more than that. The symbolism of the key was a powerful message to affirm that we all hold the key of 'positive reinforcement' within ourselves to give light and love to the world. In other words, the 'key' is our own energy field that we need to tap into and release into our world.

We stood in silence as our prayers scattered on the wings of our butterfly and through the air that gently embraced the mystical rocks for miles around. It was here where I sprinkled the water from Moses' spring as a gesture to spiritually connect the two brothers, Aaron and Moses. I was fulfilled with a sense of knowing and it was overwhelming.

I finally reached the base of Jabal Haroun with the aid of my walking stick and the arm of Nisreen, and met up with Donna and Louise, who had walked on ahead. Much to our delight, our Bedouin guide had arranged a meal for us that was spread out on a blanket on the side of a small hill. From a distance, we could smell the familiar aromas of a home-cooked meal that seemed to energise us as we walked swiftly to the picnic – a feast for the mind, body and soul after the long but exhilarating climb up and down Jabal Haroun. We gave thanks for our many blessings and tucked into Arabic salads, chickpeas and hummus, rice and chicken and freshly baked Arabic bread. It was one of the most delicious meals I have ever had!

We arrived back at the hotel just as the sun was setting, quickly showered and checked out to begin our journey back to Amman. We all slept well that night and had no aches or pains the following day. I was not surprised, as I knew our sacred work had been ordained and that we were blessed. And then I thought back to the meditation with Anya we had experienced in the car. She told us, "Please go to your heart centre and give yourself your heart's desire, for abundance is yours." Only time will tell.

It was a most memorable trip and one that I will always treasure. Miracles do come your way; you just have to have faith and believe in the signs that the universe is sending your way.

Chapter 15

A FINAL WORD ... FOR NOW

AFTER MY NEAR-DEATH EXPERIENCE in 1976, I became aware of a new sense of purpose in this world. I suddenly felt very much alive and over the years, the more I prayed and meditated, the more I began to listen to my higher self – that gut feeling you get in the pit of your stomach. Unlimited and eternal, your higher self is a part of you that inspires and guides you with intuition. It reinforced my faith in the path I was guided to walk, which resulted in a lifelong quest to discover the deeper meaning of all things spiritual. During the years since, I have met some wonderful people and experienced some extraordinary spiritual happenings that make me feel blessed beyond words. And thus began the mission I was made aware of all those years ago, and it became my truth: to spread love and light to Mother Earth.

These spiritual experiences that have guided me throughout my life are also called synchronicities, which are not just coincidences to be ignored; they are messages from the universe that are magically arranged and aligned to give meaning and a way forward in your life. Such was the experience I had during the Covid-19 pandemic when fear of the unknown was felt throughout the world. It was as if God had given me the time to share the many spiritual blessings I have received and to give hope and healing to as many people as possible because everyone is very special; we are all part of one consciousness on Mother Earth. This experience reassured me that I was on the right path to writing this book, and my late mother, yet again – in the spirit world – gave me the faith to believe it was possible. Everything I have written in this book is my truth, as I perceive it. Although I am not a religious person who goes to church every Sunday, I do pray and I respect all religions as one.

One might think that practising the healing benefits of Reiki makes people more psychic; however, in my case, I was born with the gift of intuition and psychic abilities. Along with meditation and prayer, Reiki has enhanced my abilities and helped me feel more spiritually connected to the higher source. In the process, I am able to help others to heal with joy and empathy in my heart.

Along this mystical and magical journey of my life, which is not yet finished, I have experienced tears of joy and happiness, and sadness too. I have walked a thousand miles over magnificent mountains, through beautiful valleys and along the stunning shores of many oceans, seas and lakes; and yet I feel I have many more places to visit. I feel I am blessed with God's divine grace and energy in this beautiful world. You are, too, because everyone has the power within to find those universal energies to assist us, especially when spiritual healing is needed. You must let go of all negative thoughts, such as fear or emotional pain, and banish them from your conscious mind. This will allow divine, positive energy to help you come to terms with negative emotions so they can no longer control your life.

Do not underestimate your abilities. Remember, you were born with the greatest gift of light and that light is within you; it's called love. To honour such a gift, one has to show gratitude for the blessings life bestows on us, as it is up to each one of us to allow this gift to unfold by knowing the truth of the self. Once you understand this, you will start to feel the power of awakening, little by little; recognise this as your truth. Believe, as only then will you feel it within as you are guided on the journey to the soul. This is where you will find peace of mind waiting to help you find your true purpose in this lifetime.

As a way to thank my readers for sharing this mystical journey with me, I pass on the blessing of the power of universal life force energy that we all possess; we just have to find it within.

The following mantra spoken daily will help you manifest the changes you wish for in your life:

"I Am Light

I Am Love

I Am Truth

I Am"